Praise for

The Healing Choice

by Brenda Stoeker and Susan Allen

"A rare, close-up view of the healing journey. Brenda's and Susan's parallel journeys—of wrestling with God and of finding support in the community of women—speak of hope in the midst of brokenness, acceptance in the face of unbelievable pain. Rather than allowing the devastation to crush their lives, these bold women chose to place their broken hearts and unmet dreams in God's holy hands. With amazing vulnerability, they show how wives can restore their fractured hearts, recover shattered marriages, and find help and healing regardless of their husband's choices."

—BARBARA ROSBERG, cohost of the nationally syndicated radio show *Dr. Gary and Barb, Your Marriage Coaches* and coauthor of *Six Secrets to a Lasting Love*

"What an empowering, freeing book! In *The Healing Choice*, Brenda and Susan open their lives and share how our choice to be whole is not dependent on the actions or choices of our husbands. Healing can begin now! Your life is not on hold until your husband is free. Freedom is yours regardless of where your husband is on his journey. Brenda and Susan, thanks for reaching beyond your pain to pour life into others."

—LISA BEVERE, speaker, cofounder of Messenger International, and author of *Fight Like a Girl* and *Kissed the Girls and Made Them Cry*

"This book hits very close to home. Fred's and Clay's struggle with lust and pornography are very similar to mine. And just like Susan, my wife came to the realization that to heal from such a deception can only come from a deeper walk and intimacy with our Lord and Savior Jesus Christ. Brenda reminds all of us that nothing can separate us from the love of Christ, and no matter what horrible circumstances we may end up facing, whether a drawn-out, tragic death of a dear loved one or a husband who has broken his marriage vows time and time again, Christ ultimately provides our hope of survival. Thank you, Brenda and Susan, for sharing your hearts with us so we can see how the power of God truly transforms people here on earth."

—MICHAEL O'BRIEN, singer, songwriter, and musician, and former lead singer of Newsong

"Although it can certainly feel like an overwhelming challenge, complete forgiveness and healing *isn't* an unattainable goal. Let Brenda and Susan's insightful book walk you through the restoration process step by step. It's a journey you'll be forever glad you made."

—SHANNON ETHRIDGE, MA, best-selling author of the Every Woman's Battle series and *Completely His: Loving Jesus Without Limits*

"The Stoekers and Allens continue to provide a message of wholeness to all who have been fortunate enough to experience their writings. Their contributions to the body of Christ have been and continue to be immeasurable."

—MARK GUNGOR, author of *Laugh Your Way to a Better Marriage*

"If a spouse has tragically betrayed you, then *The Healing Choice* is one of the most important books you will ever pick up. The authors, Brenda and Susan, will sensitively come alongside you in one of the darkest times of your life and then guide you through what can be a powerfully redeeming journey. Their wisdom comes not only out of their own pain but also from the grace that helped them and those they've supported to embrace restoration and hope."

—RANDY PHILLIPS, DD, former president of Promise Keepers and president of Passage

The Healing Choice
Guidebook

Move Beyond Betrayal

...and LIVE, LOVE, and THRIVE

The Healing Choice *Guidebook*

SUSAN ALLEN

WATERBROOK
PRESS

THE HEALING CHOICE GUIDEBOOK
PUBLISHED BY WATERBROOK PRESS
12265 Oracle Boulevard, Suite 200
Colorado Springs, Colorado 80921
A division of Random House Inc.

ISBN 978-1-4000-7426-6

Published in the United States by WaterBrook Multnomah, an imprint of The Doubleday Publishing Group, a division of Random House Inc., New York.

WATERBROOK and its deer design logo are registered trademarks of WaterBrook Press.

Library of Congress Cataloging-in-Publication Data
Allen, Susan, 1954–
    The healing choice guidebook : move beyond betrayal—and live, love, and thrive / by Susan Allen. — 1st ed.
        p. cm.
    Includes index.
    ISBN 978-1-4000-7426-6
    1. Wives—Religious life. 2. Christian women—Religious life. 3. Husbands—Sexual behavior. 4. Sex—Religious aspects—Christianity. 5. Betrayal. I. Title.
    BV4528.15.A45 2008
    248.8'435—dc22

                                            2008001427

Printed in the United States of America
2008—First Edition

10 9 8 7 6 5 4 3 2 1

Contents

To every woman who travels this unintended journey.

Welcome

Welcome!

This guidebook has one aim: to help you get the most out of your choice to heal following your husband's betrayal. Reading the corresponding book, *The Healing Choice,* by my coauthor, Brenda Stoeker, and me, is a good place to start. There you'll find essential solutions for rebuilding trust in God and all relationships, regardless of what your husband has done or will do in the future. It is a unique, down-to-earth look at our experiences with marital betrayal, with advice drawn from our difficult journeys. I think you will find it an ideal first step toward receiving God's promised restoration of your heart, soul, and mind, and though it isn't critical, I highly recommend you read it before engaging with the deeper work of healing offered in this guidebook.

Whether you're exploring this book alone or in the mutual support of a women's group setting, I want the experience to be as rewarding and practical for your healing as possible. Toward this end, I recommend you choose a set time for engaging with this material during the week over the course of twelve weeks. The first chapter will get you started in understanding some of the metaphors I use throughout the book and making the most of your group time with other women on this journey.

For now, I wish you Godspeed in your healing choice, and may you find lasting healing and renewed vitality through applying the "power tools" you find here.

Preparing for the Journey

Our findings suggest that at least 70 percent of marriages are impacted by some form of betrayal of intimacy. This guidebook is for the woman whose husband has betrayed her in his heart—through his thought life, by his use of pornography, or because of his sexual behaviors outside of the marriage. It is for the woman who is faced with the reality that her most intimate earthly partner has betrayed his covenant vow to her, inflicting a deep wound. The purpose of the guidebook is to help a woman in this position to heal her brokenness and equip herself to make wise decisions for the future. Whether his betrayal involved females or his own gender, the wife has to deal with the same issues.

I, too, have walked in your shoes. In the book *The Healing Choice,* I tell of my journey from brokenness to rediscovered joy. I facilitated small-group studies for women on this subject for seven years, and many of those women's stories are woven into the pages of that book. My own learning, as well as the insights gleaned from the groups, helped to form the guidebook you have in your hands.

This material is not intended to take the place of a licensed therapist. After participating in this study, you may decide further advice from a professional counselor would be beneficial.

In *The Healing Choice* we described a husband's betrayal as an unintended journey in life, an earth-shattering life change that thrusts you into a relational wilderness without warning, and often without adequate spiritual and emotional resources. Angie was one who experienced such a journey:

I am desperate for a pinpoint of hope right now. Though I am just married, my husband's porn and lust is killing our marriage. I have been so completely deceived and lied to that I've become someone else, someone I don't want to be. I have never been so hurt, wounded, frustrated, and hopeless. My husband is a believer and knows all the right words to say about this issue, but the sin continues daily (if not hourly), and he continues to lie to me about it and to deceive himself by saying he "isn't as bad as the next guy." We have been to counseling, but that only worked for a day.

I can no longer handle this issue on my own. I am desperate for someone to show my husband the depth and weight of his sin. I need encouragement and counseling myself. This is a nightmare compared to my Christian dreams of marriage. I had no idea what I was getting myself into when I said, "I do."

If you are becoming someone *you* don't want to be on this unintended journey, working through this guidebook should be a good first step toward transforming into the woman you were meant to be. By God's truth and grace, you don't have to wait for your husband to change. You can restore your heart today, even now.

Of course, as Brenda writes, there *will* be challenges along the way:

I write with no illusions, because I understand that forgiving a deep sexual betrayal comes with great difficulty—especially when you aren't sure what repentance ought to look like and there is no guarantee that your husband won't commit the same sins again. He's been lying and hiding. How can you be sure this nightmare is over? (*Every Heart Restored,* 3)

But in spite of these challenges, your heart *can* heal completely right in the middle of the nightmare, whether your husband repents or not. It may not feel that way at the moment, but it's true. You are not without hope. God is at your side, hoping you'll find some sisters to walk with you:

Brethren, if any person is overtaken in misconduct or sin of any sort, you who are spiritual [who are responsive to and controlled by the Spirit] should set him right and restore and reinstate him, without any sense of superiority and with all gentleness, keeping an attentive eye on yourself, lest you should be tempted also.

Bear (endure, carry) one another's burdens and troublesome moral faults, and in this way fulfill and observe perfectly the law of Christ (the Messiah) and complete what is lacking [in your obedience to it]. (Galatians 6:1–2, AMP)

If there's ever been an answer to how to respond to a husband's sexual sin, this is it. Finding community among your sisters in Christ allows you to share your commonalities and difficulties. By using these curricula and the resources I've put in place for you, I believe you will survive and even thrive on this journey.

Throughout this guide I use several analogies to help paint the picture of this unintended journey you will traverse:

- *Landmarks.* Each chapter in the guidebook acts as a landmark to help you clearly recognize the place you are, like a YOU ARE HERE cue on a map. Those who have been there before you provide you with bearings for guidance. The landmarks will help you focus your attention on specific aspects of the new terrain you'll travel over the twelve weeks of the study.

- *My Stone Work.* These sections point to the specific work you have to do along the journey, the stones dotting the path that you need to stop and consider for your own personal growth, decisions, and healing. Those labeled *Insight* will help you identify the stones and prompt you to make a plan for dealing with them appropriately. Those labeled *Action* are intended to guide you in taking definitive steps in spiritual growth, emotional healing, and the restoration of your entire being. Some of your work will be long-term and intensive. But if you keep forging through your stone work, you won't become bogged down or stuck.

- *Walking Companions.* "All the believers met together constantly and shared everything with each other" (Acts 2:44). More than anything else, you need the fellowship of other women who will hold your hand, listen, and consider your stones with you. With other women, you'll end isolation and shame, and you'll broaden your understanding in safety. Ultimately, how much you share in your group is up to you. You can find out more about locating an Avenue group or creating your own by visiting our Web site at AvenueResource.com or by calling our confidential call center at 1-877-326-7000.

Suggestions to Maximize Healing

- Find or initiate a small group to walk through this study together.
- Learn to listen and obey God's promptings by establishing a regular time of daily prayer and Bible reading.
- Journal thoughts, prayers, and decisions as they unfold.
- Complete the suggested stone work sections.
- Attend your group each week.
- Call the women in your group midweek for prayer and emotional support.
- Attend a church for spiritual nourishment.

At the end of most chapters, further resources are provided. Take advantage of these if you sense a need for further help on specific issues. I especially recommend the WaterBrook books written by Fred Stoeker, the primary author of the award-winning Every Man series. I recommend *Every Man's Battle, Every Man's Challenge,* and *Tactics* for husbands, and *Every Heart Restored* and *The Healing Choice* for wives. However, for your first time through the study, focusing on the stone work will be the most beneficial use of your time.

Why Journal?

Many women consider the journaling habit one of the main reasons for their spiritual success. When you consider the benefits, it's easy to see why:

- Journaling encourages thoroughness. Unexamined thoughts lead to unrealized growth. Capturing your thoughts helps you escape worry and fear.
- Journaling about your state of mind helps you sort through what is going on in your life and gain balance and control.
- Journaling aids your memory and marks your progress as your circumstances change.
- Journaling provides another opportunity for God to speak to you.
- Journaling encourages greater objectivity about your own thoughts and feelings.

- Journaling helps you document God's answers to your prayers.
- Journaling can sustain you when you feel weary on the journey.
- Journaling can become a testimony to others in need.

In my experience, the woman who writes in tears today will eventually read back over her journal in joy.

Group Courtesies

1. Attend regularly. Commit to weekly attendance, and contact your facilitator when you need to be absent.
2. Respect confidentiality. Do not discuss others' issues outside the group.
3. Keep discussion voluntary. But challenge yourself to share, as each woman's personal insights can benefit the group.
4. Avoid giving advice, and do not try to solve others' problems. Use "I" sentences, not "you" or "your."
5. Do not monopolize conversation. Get to the heart of what you want to say. Then respect others by listening attentively.
6. Do not fixate on others' issues. Focus on your own growth.
7. Use prayer time for healing work. Limit group prayer time to issues pertaining to marriage and personal healing for you and others affected.
8. Respect differences. Embracing differences is a key strength of any group. Encourage rather than compare yourself with others.
9. Acknowledge commonality. Regardless of details, work toward unity within this common issue.
10. Commit to do your stone work, as it will benefit the entire group.
11. Stick to the guidebook; don't discuss other books or workshop material. It will focus your group time and eliminate distractions.
12. Clearly distinguish the facilitator's role. Instead of acting as a counselor or teacher, the facilitator should guide group time, initiate prayer, direct discussion, and remind everyone of courtesies.
13. Invite feedback. Encourage a safe, open atmosphere, and share evaluations of the group's strengths and weaknesses.

First Landmark

Reeling from Shock to Anger

Save me, O my God.... Deeper and deeper I sink in the
mire.... I have wept until I am exhausted; my throat is dry
and hoarse; my eyes are swollen with weeping, waiting for
my God to act.... Save me from the pit that threatens
me.... Rescue me, O God, from my poverty and pain.

PSALM 69:1–3, 15, 29

When we enter into love, we are ever at risk of losing it. In love, we must be willing to be vulnerable, and that willingness opens the gateway to suffering the loss of that love. What we lose in love may come through tragedy, decay, neglect, or compromise, yet "the LORD is close to the brokenhearted and saves those who are crushed in spirit" (Psalm 34:18, NIV).

The emotions a woman experiences upon discovery of a husband's betrayal are similar to the grief, anguish, and chaos experienced upon the death of a loved one. In fact, that is why we spent the first half of *The Healing Choice* discussing the parallels between the losses from grieving a death and the losses from sexual betrayal. The loss of a relationship, the uncertainty of the future, the sudden detour of life, and the intensity of the reactions are all common and often follow a predictable sequence. Yet no journey to healing follows a straight line. Women usually bounce between emotions, revisiting difficult paths they thought they'd left behind. Studies tell us it is unusual *not* to experience intense and fluctuating emotions to some degree in the aftermath of a husband's betrayal.

Though difficult and emotionally demanding, stumbling through and enduring the emotional switchbacks along this stone-pocked road is the only way to spiritual and emotional recovery. The typical sequence of stones that appear in the path are shock, denial, anger, blame, mourning, chaos, acceptance, and finally hope.

We will focus on each of these individually in the next two chapters, adding one more emotion exclusive to your particular circumstance: jealousy. Another common emotion accompanying this journey is fear. We will devote a later chapter to this big stumbling stone.

Shock

> I weep for the hurt of my [daughter]; I stand amazed, silent, dumb with grief.
> (Jeremiah 8:21)

The dictionary defines *shock* as "a sudden arousing of emotion or disturbance of mental stability by something unexpected, offensive, or unwelcome." It is often accompanied by physical symptoms including lightheadedness, nausea, diarrhea, pain, or feeling like you've been hit in the stomach. There may be an adrenaline rush or loss of appetite as well.

For most women who face a husband's betrayal, no definition of *shock* is necessary. Heidi understood shock up close and personal when she was betrayed by her husband, Michael O'Brien, former lead singer of the Grammy Award–winning group NewSong.

> "Dear Lord God!" I cried aloud as I attempted to muffle the sound with my pillow. "I don't understand. I just don't understand!" I had shut my bedroom door in retreat, farther still into my bathroom, and finally my closet—locking the door behind me, trying to reach some womblike comfort. There wasn't a hole deep enough, and no matter how far I shoved my head in the sand, nothing would make the truth go away. Surrounded by discarded clothes and clutter, I hugged tight to my pillow and wept. *Betrayed!* I thought. *All these years, lie after lie! What else has he been lying to me about? Oh, Jesus!*

"I'm going to throw up!" I moaned. Another voice inside scolded, *Oh, Heidi, you are so dramatic! It is not as if he actually had an affair!*

"It sure feels like it!" I cried. *How exactly am I supposed to do life today… grocery shopping, breakfast, laundry? How am I supposed to function when I am emotionally hemorrhaging?*

Michael said he would make an appointment with our pastor, but it wouldn't be soon enough. How would I survive until then? What was he thinking anyway? As if he could give me some pill, say a prayer, wave a magic wand, and make everything go away! I just wanted the world to freeze until I could sort this all out.

Shock can proceed quickly to numbness, which acts as a defense against overwhelming emotion and gives the body time to assimilate. This stage is usually short lived, from several days to several weeks, and subsides naturally.

Denial

Get the facts at any price, and hold on tightly to all the good sense you can get. (Proverbs 23:23)

Denial is "an assertion that something is not true, a refusal to acknowledge a truth." Denial is a common, usually short-lived disbelief in response to an unacceptable new reality.

Denial can sometimes be prolonged. If a widow is still setting a place at the table for her husband months after his death, she is remaining in denial purposefully through constant maintenance. Prolonged denial demands disregarding intuitive knowledge and evidence that contradicts the make-believe world of denial. It is always healthier to face facts, but avoidance of reality has its benefits. Addressing the truth may be too difficult, too costly, or too painful.

Yet nongrowth is a very unhealthy place to stay. Prolonged denial can bring depression, despair, even panic disorders. A woman may become hyperactive in housecleaning, in her job, or in other activities, staying overly busy and preoccupied to avoid seeing the truth.

MY · STONE · WORK

Insight

Denial can be particularly difficult to shake. Even after you've faced the enormous truth, smaller stones may remain hidden behind denial. You may have focused on creating a path around the biggest stone and forgotten the related truths that also need to be faced.

Start to clear away any remaining denial by journaling about how your husband's actions and attitudes have harmed you. Then step bravely forward to ask a woman you trust to look at your pages. Maybe she's your walking companion. Ask her to look for things you may have unconsciously or purposely left out. Then write down her observations. To stay firmly grounded in reality, revisit this entry throughout your journey.

Action

Seek accountability from your walking companions about any remaining denial. Invite open feedback on your thinking. Bring your thoughts before God, asking Him to continually open your eyes to the truth.

Blame

We can always "prove" that we are right, but is the Lord convinced? (Proverbs 16:2)

Blame means "to hold responsible, lay the fault for responsibility for something wrong or unsatisfactory." Blame, while a common defense, is misplaced in regard to a husband's betrayal. A woman looking for a scapegoat for her husband's actions may say things like, "She came on to him," "Porn is inescapable," or even, "If only I'd..., he wouldn't have needed that." Facing the real issue in your marriage requires you to stop blaming others or yourself for your husband's betrayal. Your husband's behavior is his to control, no one else's. To heal, you must deal with reality, and misplacing blame impedes this process. No one but your husband has the responsibility and power to deal with his own sin.

Anger

> If you are angry, don't sin by nursing your grudge. Don't let the sun go down
> with you still angry—get over it quickly; for when you are angry you give a
> mighty foothold to the devil. (Ephesians 4:26–27)

Anger means "passionate displeasure." It is a natural reaction to being hurt. Realization of such personal deceit is enough to enrage even mild-mannered women. Often women say that after learning of their husbands' betrayal, the entire relationship felt like a fraud, as though the marriage were canceled out. A woman may revisit anger repeatedly when facing the myriad losses her husband's behavior has cost her or her family. You may even feel angry at yourself:

> What could be more normal? When you find out [what your husband has been
> doing], you'll feel utterly blindsided. You may even be kicking yourself for not
> having seen it coming, especially if your female intuition sent out early warning
> signals…signals that you, in your faithfulness to him, laughed off as paranoid or
> even out-and-out silly. (*Every Heart Restored*, 26)

Anger is a God-given emotion, but it must be properly managed. Anger must be dealt with swiftly and directly. God's response of righteous anger is seen in the story of Hosea and Gomer when God made His feelings known about Gomer's promiscuous behavior (see Hosea 2). Similarly, there is no benefit in shielding your husband from your feelings. If he is to repent, he needs to see the depth of your pain. Processing your anger is necessary for both of you to heal. During the first few days after discovering the betrayal, the intensity of rage can be terrifying. You may sense you are losing control. This is a dangerous time. Righteous anger, on the other hand, never controls us. Appropriate, righteous anger never inflicts injury on others or intends to do damage.

But when a woman is trapped in denial, blame, crippling neediness, or paralyzing fear, she may create a barrier to expressing proper anger. Women who cannot process and express anger at all are headed for depression. The Ephesians verse quoted previously instructs that expressing anger immediately and directly to the object of your anger is necessary to *progress* rather than *repress*. The verses emphasize that it's holding on to and dwelling on your anger that produces harm.

Women who use anger as a weapon are often trying to protect more vulnerable feelings of inadequacy, shame, and fear. Moving past anger is vital to restoring emotional balance and health, so all emotions can be expressed and processed progressively and fully.

The surge of energy that comes with anger can be constructive rather than destructive when you apply it to your recovery work and seek God's voice. If you need a physical release, exercising, purging a cluttered closet, or smacking the sofa with a bat can help release some of the overflow of aggression. When you are honest about your feelings and choose God's healing for your life, anger always subsides. That doesn't mean it is always gone for good. After several good days, something triggers your anger again. But there will be complete healing as you repeatedly submit your anger to God.

MY · STONE · WORK

Insight

If you are unable to express your anger without rage, you may find it helpful to write a letter to your husband. Once you have written your letter, read it aloud in private to God. Ask Him to help you communicate your anger without being destructive. After working through these emotions with God, you may decide to rewrite your letter before sharing it with your husband.

Action

Communicating your anger to your husband is rarely met with enthusiasm, but if he has sought forgiveness, he will likely hear you out. Don't come with expectations about how he should respond. This information can send him into deeper shame, and it may be met with silence or even defensive anger. He will need time to process your feelings with his own. Yet honesty and sincerity brought in a spirit of constructive effort can begin healing for both of you.

The letter should not be a substitute for direct communication with your husband, unless you are concerned for your safety or he is simply not willing to listen. In either of these cases, you may consider the "empty chair" approach. Sit opposite an empty chair that represents your absent husband, and read the letter aloud as if he were there. Decide whether to keep the letter for the future possibility of talking face to face.

Release the anger and bring your hurts to God. Finally, in order to not "let the sun go down with you still angry," it's vital to apply this instruction: "Lie quietly upon your bed in silent meditation.... I will lie down in peace and sleep, for though I am alone, O Lord, you will keep me safe" (Psalm 4:4, 8). Though you may kick up new pebbles of anger tomorrow, God wants you to lean into Him for comfort, allowing Him to hold your cares while you take needed rest.

Jealousy

Jealousy is more dangerous and cruel than anger. (Proverbs 27:4)

The dictionary defines *jealous* as "fearful or wary of being supplanted; apprehensive of losing affection or position; vigilant in guarding something." This is one emotion that differs from that of losing love through death. It is a huge emotion. Who doesn't feel jealous when the one she loves is untrue? Sometimes jealousy is born of insecurity. Sometimes it's the most rational feeling you could experience. Yet it makes us feel small, anxious, and childlike. And depending on one's personality, it can stir up fear or anger or both.

Jealousy is also a God-given emotion, and in the Old Testament, God speaks of His jealousy when His children turn their backs on Him. "The Holy Spirit, whom God has placed within us, watches over us with tender jealousy" (James 4:5). This kind of jealousy seeks to protect the love it owns. That ownership is right, pure, and motivated by love. Threats and intrusions to that ownership naturally cause jealousy, as God experienced when His children became smitten by other gods: "They have made me very jealous of their idols, which are not gods at all" (Deuteronomy 32:21). Just as God was jealous of His people's worship of other gods, women who have been betrayed feel jealous; they have a right to feel jealous and should not be blamed for feeling that way. Any betrayal of trust warrants increased vigilance in guarding your marriage. Yet at the same time, we are called not to cling, smother, or control any relationship selfishly. Remember: "Love is very patient and kind, never jealous or envious" (1 Corinthians 13:4).

Reign in any jealousy born of insecurity. If you notice you are jealous of another's looks, you may need to reassess your values. Just because a provocative person is present in a room doesn't mean your husband is doing anything wrong. You need to weed out your own insecurity from the true threats and maturely assess your and your husband's healthy and unhealthy relationships.

Potentially compromising situations should be eliminated. Work relationships that start out healthy but without proper boundaries can become inappropriately intimate and secretive. "Work" lunches may or may not be business lunches. Husbands and wives should observe appropriate boundaries to avoid potential compromise. We'll discuss healthy boundaries further in a later chapter.

My Prayer for My Emotions

Lord, take my broken heart and calm my restless soul. Renew me in Your Spirit and teach me to hope again. Help me to see beyond the pain. Show me how to deal with my anger and tears. And use my hurts to teach me compassion toward others who are wounded. In the name of Jesus, amen.

Further Resources
Torn Asunder: Recovering from Extramarital Affairs, Dave Carder (Chicago: Moody, 1992).

Second Landmark

Moving from Mourning to Hope

He reached down from heaven and took me and drew me
out of my great trials. He rescued me from deep waters....
He led me to a place of safety, for he delights in me.

PSALM 18:16, 19

The dictionary defines *mourn* as "to express or feel grief." When I first encountered deep grief, I was struck by how callously the world goes on as if nothing has changed. As I awoke each morning, I was freshly reminded that my whole world had turned up-side down. Yet the trash man and the paperboy went about their daily routines, and everyone rushed to work, completely oblivious to my grief. I was completely and utterly alone in my suffering. And the loneliness was even more pronounced, since I did not allow God into my life. I no longer live in that dreadful place, and I am grate-ful, but even when God is in our lives, He does not erase the loneliness we experience in mourning. One woman expressed it this way:

How can a person who is so in touch with reality live so many hours outside of
that reality? The answer is grief...it makes everything in life seem so fuzzy that it
blurs the line between what's real and what isn't...it is the unwanted companion
who has intruded upon my life...an uninvited guest. Grief shows up at the most

inopportune times, so unexpectedly. It makes my eyes burn with tears…it causes my heart to ache, my stomach to lurch, my throat to close up, and random thoughts to come tumbling out of my mind…memories that I don't want to think about…and then come the tears, slowly at first…then streaming until I am sobbing uncontrollably and feel like I'm drowning and there is no comfort or consolation, and no one to save me. After what seems like hours, I remember that I need to get ready for work. I need to put my thoughts aside and walk to the bathroom to begin another day in this dead world, only a shadow of the real one… Your world, Lord, heaven…the one I can almost touch when I am full of the grief.

"In my alarm I said, 'I am cut off from your sight!' Yet you heard my cry for mercy when I called to you for help. Love the LORD, all his saints! The LORD preserves the faithful, but the proud he pays back in full. Be strong and take heart, all you who hope in the LORD" (Psalm 31:22–24, NIV). The last lines in this psalm are the reason I don't relive my own grief when seeing someone else's. Beyond mourning, I always see the hope she cannot yet see for herself. I remember my pain, but I don't live there any longer. God plants seeds of hope in every situation. But that doesn't immediately alleviate the pain that at times can seem unbearable. No one experienced grief more intensely than Jesus when He cried out in deep despair, "My God, my God, why have you forsaken me?" (Matthew 27:46). Strong feeling may come crashing like waves, pulling us down again with each new crest. Pain can begin to feel like a permanent condition. We lose hope of ever feeling better or even that God wants to free us. But give yourself time. Be patient with your fluctuating emotions. When the unbearable pain becomes so familiar, you may feel like you want to bury it or run from it. But know that He has a cure and avoiding it only prolongs the pain.

Emotions will not stay buried, except under a blanket of depression. Stay present in your pain. Do not run from strong emotions, but allow them to surface. Experience and connect with the world around you, and allow God to access your wound. Our emotions aren't cured by negating them or by thinking positive thoughts. We are to bring our thoughts and emotions to God, giving Him permission to do the supernatural work of healing that only He can do. Though at times your emotions' intensity may frighten you, the chaos will calm as you allow God to do the real work of healing.

MY · STONE · WORK

Insight

Write about what you lost as a result of your husband's betrayal and about the grief you feel because of what's been stolen from you: promises, hopes, and opportunities. It may take some time, but continue to add to your list over the weeks of this study as you recognize more losses.

Action

Grief doesn't arrive when it's convenient. You might find yourself at your desk at work or hosting your child's birthday party when a triggered memory overwhelms you with grief. In some situations, you may need to stifle your feelings, but you need to return to them in private. Make these times a priority. Your grief may not be present when you get alone, but take time to read through your losses, talk to God about your disappointments, and face your difficult emotions openly before God. At first it may feel forced, but remember that you are giving yourself a rest from busyness to take care of your broken heart.

   Just as with your communication of anger, voicing to your spouse the losses you're grieving is never pleasant, but it is another important step toward healing. This conversation can wait though. Over the coming months of this study, continue to add to your "loss list" as more losses surface. You will utilize this list in a later chapter to communicate with your husband.

Emotional Chaos

Chaos is defined as "a condition or place of great disorder or confusion." Picture a massive windstorm tearing the roof off your house. Life as you knew it has been turned on its head. You've lost your bearings; your house is no longer stable, certain, or dependable.

Following your husband's betrayal, all the rules have changed. What you once relied on has evaporated. Though you struggle to move forward, you're confused, aimless. With so much out of place and unsettled, you might experience mental confusion. The problem of chaos is twofold: the chaos of your circumstances and the internal chaos of your emotions. Most women experience a loss of confidence, sense of self, and strength of purpose.

Furthermore, this season of chaos doesn't vaporize on its own. Emotionally, it can be a dangerous time. You might be tempted to numb the cacophony with denial, blame, substance abuse, or irrational behavior.

Even if you're determined to work through the chaos, where do you start when so much is in disarray? Throughout this study, as you encounter landmarks along this well-marked path, you'll find help to clean up the mess, learning what to keep and what needs to be thrown away.

So now, with confidence that what you're facing is normal and can be overcome, let's turn the corner and see what lies beyond these emotional stones.

Acceptance

Acceptance means "to admit the truth." Acceptance is *not* agreeing with or being happy about reality. It is simply acknowledging that the current circumstance *is* reality. It involves dropping "what if" thinking. There are three realities involved in acceptance:

1. The reality of the situation. "You will know the truth, and the truth will set you free" (John 8:32). Beyond denial and blame, we may still despise our situation. But coming to terms that this *is* our new reality can be the starting point for positive, progressive changes for ourselves, our children, and our marriages. Part of acceptance is acknowledging that pain *and* gain are a package deal.

2. The reality of our fallen world. "I have told you all this so that you will have peace of heart and mind. Here on earth you will have many trials and sorrows; but cheer up, for I have overcome the world" (John 16:33). God has laid out for us in the Bible how life really is—and it's no fairy tale! Acknowledge once and for all that life isn't fair. Accept that it isn't the happily ever after we all long for. Give up your illusions, and you will realize that what Jesus said about this life is true.

3. The reality of God's peace. "I am leaving you with a gift—peace of mind and heart! And the peace I give isn't fragile like the peace the world gives. So don't be troubled or afraid" (John 14:27). When we start believing His Word and following it as our guide to life, we discover that life, relationship, purpose, and peace are all guaranteed. This knowledge is the source of power to restore our losses and heal our hearts.

Hope

"I know the plans I have for you," declares the LORD, "plans to prosper you and not to harm you, plans to give you hope and a future." (Jeremiah 29:11, NIV)

Hope means "to place trust in, to rely on." If you have grasped even a glimmer of hope for your circumstances, you know that it changes everything. You become thankful again for each new day instead of greeting the morning with dread. And you have every reason to trust God for better things in your future circumstances.

When we make the decision to stop hoping, we end up in deep despair. We may have discovered through disappointment how dangerous it is to hope. We may not want to hope for our husbands to change. We may believe it's easier to let the marriage die than risk being hurt again. But the unfortunate by-product of that way of thinking is despair and a hardened heart that can no longer experience true joy: "Hope deferred makes the heart sick" (Proverbs 13:12).

You have the choice to hope beyond your present situation. God wants to renew your hope and your circumstances, and though no one knows how long it will take, if you put your hope in God rather than in your circumstances, your hope and joy in life will eventually return. Life after loss is never the same, but deep, positive change will take place if you face the aftermath grounded in hope.

I have seen women renewed to completely restored lives—marriages redeemed and brokenness healed. Other women have found new hope in being single, and God has replaced their loss with a new freedom, a new relationship with Him, and new friendships. I've even seen God heal the wounds that these women had been carrying since childhood. He'll do it for you too, if you give Him the chance:

There's no shame in wounds. Was it child abuse? your dad's verbal battering? date rape? Perhaps you've become a great actress, hiding your pain from the world, but out here in the valley of wilderness, your haunting cry can no longer be silenced. Your husband's betrayal has those old feelings of defenselessness and fear bubbling over again as if all of it happened yesterday.

Isn't it time for that healing? Of course, you *will* have to finally let go of those losses and be willing to trade them for the gifts God wants to give you. Unlike people, He cannot violate your free will. But if you will let go of your "right" to harbor offense in your heart, you will create a place for joy. It's a worthwhile trade. Give Him your old, tattered box of broken dreams, and let Him hand you a renewed heart full of new, wondrous dreams: "I will give you one heart and a new spirit; I will take from you your hearts of stone and give you tender hearts of love for God" (Ezekiel 11:19). "When dreams come true at last, there is life and joy" (Proverbs 13:12).

Emotions are a mixed bag. Some are welcome; some are uninvited. They can change moment to moment. But may we allow our emotions to change our nature. May grief help us to appreciate joy, increase our thankfulness, and help us become more sensitive to others who suffer. May our response to pain allow God to perfect us, to replace any lack in our hearts with fullness. May we allow our trials to grow us and strengthen our character, so we can agree with this scripture:

> We are able to hold our heads high no matter what happens and know that all is well, for we know how dearly God loves us, and we feel this warm love everywhere within us because God has given us the Holy Spirit to fill our hearts with his love. (Romans 5:5)

My Prayer for a Broken Heart

Lord, heal my grief. I can't climb out of this darkness without You.
I need Your perspective to transpose mine. Give me strength to care
for the daily things that can't be put on hold. Help me find the time

*to grieve in the midst of my life. Allow Your words of hope to pene-
trate my soul. Remind me that all things are possible with You.
Help me seek out the help You send for me. You made me, Lord; I
know You will show me how to move from heartbreak to hope. In
Jesus's name, amen.*

. . . .

Further Resources
On mourning: *The Healing Choice,* Brenda Stoeker and Susan Allen (Colorado
    Springs: WaterBrook, 2008).
On emotions: *The Cry of the Soul,* Dan Allender and Tremper Longman III (Colorado
    Springs: NavPress, 1994).

Third Landmark

Red Flags

Can't you hear the voice of wisdom? She is standing at
the city gates and at every fork in the road…. "Listen,
[women]!" she calls. "…Let me give you understanding."

PROVERBS 8:1, 4–5

For years I picked up occasional warning signs of my husband's sexual sin, but I was naive and uninformed, and I wasn't certain that these signs were adding up to anything serious. I didn't rely on my conscience and intuition.

It is impossible to discern the truth about your husband's betrayal while being supplied only with half truths and lies, so if you missed it, don't feel silly or foolish. You simply didn't have all the information. Most sexual betrayal is practiced in secret and can be hidden even more easily than other destructive behaviors. This is why it's of paramount importance to be aware of what you do see and learn what's really going on, especially if you suspect he may be at it again.

Clear signs of sexual betrayal include evidence of pornographic material and frequent excuses about it, demands for degrading sex acts in your marriage bed, and frequent masturbation. Following are two lists of the less obvious indicators or symptoms of sexual betrayal. Note that none of these signs alone proves your husband is being unfaithful. But if you've noticed at least two or three of these over a short period of time, there is reason for concern. Note also that you should never need to nag, trail him, or snoop.

These signs are observable in everyday life. They may point to other or additional issues—all serious problems—such as drugs or alcohol use, gambling, workaholism, or anger. Yet if he is not willing to be accountable for his time, expenditures, and behavior to his wife, or if his actions are unloving, disrespectful, or deceitful, he is showing clear signs of a deeper issue.

Classic Signs of Sexual Betrayal

- He is unaccountable for time away from home and how he spends his money.
- He works late, travels often, and is difficult to reach.
- He will not commit to regular arrival times.
- He avoids answering his cell phone.
- He seems distant, mentally preoccupied.
- He spends a lot of time on the Internet and/or refuses to use a filtering service.
- He watches television or uses the computer after you go to bed.
- He misses sleep or gets up regularly in the middle of the night.
- You have debts that he isn't concerned about.
- You've found unusual receipts, phone numbers, phone bills, or credit charges.
- He has unpredictable moods, including anger and depression.
- He blames you for his unhappiness, anger, and/or shortcomings.
- His sexual interest in you has waned or increased dramatically.
- He does not want intimacy yet demands sexual acts that are unpleasant.
- He has grown emotionally distant from friends and family.
- He says you're crazy, jealous, or have a vivid imagination.
- He demands certain sexual performances and gets upset when refused.
- You feel used, empty, during or after sex.
- You've regularly considered whether or not he is lying to you.

Classic Signs of an Affair

- He spends less time with you than he used to—with explanations of work, business functions, a new hobby, or a sport.
- He's less affectionate.

- He changes his looks, style, hair, cologne, exercise habits.
- He's more short-tempered.
- He's defensive about his schedule.
- He becomes private about his cell phone, computer, and finances.

Remember that as you check off his behaviors on these lists, none of the attitudes or actions are a clear indicator of sexual betrayal. But if you find that many of these things are true of him, it points to a high probability. It is critical that you avoid denial, and these red flags will help you do so, by God's grace.

You'll need God's discernment to see through your husband's bluster as he tries to wriggle out of the light. That bluster can cause many wives to believe their husbands' excuses, which is a form of denial.

As you may know, there can be an overwhelming urge to sweep everything under your heart's rug and to bury the emotion of it all. Like the heartrending scene from *Gone with the Wind,* you naively trust that everything will work out somehow, passionately muttering like Scarlett O'Hara, "I can't think about this today… I'll go crazy if I do. I'll think about it tomorrow."

God already has one naive, blind, broken child on the scene in the form of your husband, and He can't afford to have two. He's asking you to move in closer to Him so He might make your sight completely whole. He needs one trust-worthy child on hand to work with Him in this, and He wants to make you strong. (*Every Heart Restored,* 184)

MY · STONE · WORK

Insight

If you believe your husband is betraying you (again or still), you need to consider some boundary issues: Do you know how you want to be treated? Does your husband's behavior offend you? Do you realize you are right and justified for feeling hurt? Has he broken your trust repeatedly? Do you commonly give him second, third, and fourth chances? Journal your insights.

Action

If the signs you recognize are the same as those you saw in the past, he may be betraying you again. This is not a time for thinking he's innocent until proven guilty. Most spouses never have 100 percent proof without a full confession. Though you may not have all the details and may not want them, acknowledging that something is terribly amiss is critical.

If you're facing this common circumstance, follow these steps:

- Thank God for revealing these signs to you.
- Pray for wisdom to determine a godly response.
- Discuss the situation and pray with your group or walking companion.
- Enforce the appropriate consequences.

If you have been living without boundaries, you may not feel comfortable enforcing consequences or even know what they might be. We'll deal with this in later chapters.

Repairing Your Intuition and Conscience

The dictionary defines *intuition* as "direct perception of truth, fact, etc., independent of any reasoning process." *Conscience* is "the inner sense of what is right or wrong in one's conduct or motives, impelling one toward right action."

In Romans 1:19–20, Paul describes how every human being intuitively knows there is a God without being told, simply by looking at creation. Paul goes on to say that even without formal instruction, people have a sense, or a conscience, that informs them what is right and wrong. When we try to brush that knowledge aside, we become fools.

Instinct and conscience are parts of our inherent sensory makeup—just as real as our senses of sight and smell. We often describe them as "gut feelings." Yet if we ignore them or handle them incorrectly, we can sometimes lose the use of them.

For instance, we can talk ourselves into believing lies. To see evil and accept it, we have to tell our consciences to be quiet. Do this often enough, and these God-given senses become numb. From this state of numbness, we can easily miss information and make costly errors in judgment. Typically, we silence our instinct and conscience in response to fear, to keep the peace, or to avoid facing an unpleasant reality.

MY · STONE · WORK

Insight

If you suspect you are out of touch with what your conscience and intuition are trying to tell you, go back through your relational history—your husband, previous boyfriends, family of origin—and consider times when you were conflicted about what your conscience and/or instincts were telling you. Write in your journal any old situations that confirm your intuition was telling the truth.

Action

Rely on yourself, your group, and your walking companion by being honest about your concerns. All can help you regain your internal senses and shed light on things that are difficult to look at. When you begin doubting yourself again, refer to your journal, and write down the red flags you encounter.

Addressing Other Problems

My husband, Clay, struggled with other problems as well. One was money. Like sex, spending was a medication for him. He didn't want to hear the word *budget*. It was too stifling to him. He was living in a make-believe world of "I can have what I want when I want it," and I went along passively—for too long.

I have met many women who said that sexual betrayal was not the only problem they faced with their mates. There were others that came with it:

- gambling
- sports obsession

- workaholism
- drug or alcohol abuse
- overspending
- obsessive television or movie watching
- Internet addiction

Some women were not even aware of their spouses' sexual misbehavior because they could not see past the other, more visible problems or obsessions. One of the things that blinded me to my husband's sexual betrayal was his addiction to work. His one day off would usually begin with his taking care of "just one more thing at work" that would last until two in the afternoon or later.

The common denominator in all of these behaviors is that they serve to medicate pain—or even just disappointment over the everydayness of life. They are the man's attempt to alter or escape the reality he feels he cannot face otherwise.

Often people with compulsions have more than one, a kind of backup system. And multiple behaviors can reinforce one another. Frequently, only one will be obvious. For the habitual offender, this can help hide the larger, foundational problem.

Yet to be healed, all compulsive behaviors need to be addressed. Like a stack of blocks after the bottom one is pulled out, the complex structure of compulsive behaviors crumbles when one compulsion is revealed and the rest can no longer be maintained. When drugs and alcohol are a problem, these are the first blocks that have to come down. Anger is another block. While substance addiction creates varied barriers to dealing with deeper behavioral issues, anger creates barriers through control, projection, and manipulation. And the power anger supplies can be just as addictive as any substance.

Barriers set up by a variety of behaviors often hide the one root issue. In *Every Heart Restored,* Fred and Brenda tell the story of Fred's harsh temper early in their marriage. In his book *Tactics,* Fred dissects the wounds underlying his sexual sin. Both of these compulsions grew out of the father wounds Fred endured as a child—his temper and his sexual sin provided a sense of control and became emotional medication. To free himself and restore their marriage, Fred had to deal with all the issues—the temper, the sexual sin, and the father wounds.

That's how it is for everyone. Eventually, all the blocks must come down. If they don't, the addict merely shifts to another medication. People who quit smoking only to put on thirty pounds are a good example of this. A "dry drunk" may have quit drinking but hasn't dealt with the issues that brought on the drinking in the first place. Until the causes are dealt with, even a "sober" sex addict can't experience true healing and intimacy.

Maybe you are aware of your spouse's related addictions. Maybe you told yourself if he stopped being unfaithful, that would be good enough. But his addictions prove there are still big issues to be dealt with. And left unaddressed, the issues will continue to threaten your marriage and family.

Your spouse may have begun sleeping around because of his drinking, or he may have had an affair because of long hours with that woman at the office. Nonetheless, whether it's one addictive behavior or another, it's still a substitute for reality.

Many men with sexual compulsivity have jobs that offer freedom to come and go without much accountability—sales jobs with frequent travel, self-employment, service and consulting jobs. Wives, make it your business to become aware of related habits and compromising behaviors. Do not dismiss the evidence; allow your intuition to talk to you.

MY · STONE · WORK

Insight

Do you see multiple signs or patterns of behavior in your husband's life? Write in your journal anything your intuition is telling you.

Action

Walking toward emotional health means addressing your spouse's other problems along with his sexual behavior. God will help you as you courageously peel back the layers of addiction to get at the root issue…one at a time.

My Prayer for My Response to Red Flags

Open my eyes, Lord, to see what You want to show me. Prepare my heart, Lord, to respond to these truths in love. Give me wisdom and discernment, that I may not be deceived. Give me courage to take loving action and not run away in fear. I bind the spirit of fear that would keep me from walking on the pathway that You have set before me. In Jesus Christ's name, amen.

Further Resources

Don't Call It Love: Recovery from Sexual Addition, Patrick Carnes, PhD (New York: Bantam, 1992).

Angry Men and the Women Who Love Them, Paul Hegstrom (Kansas City, MO: Beacon Hill, 2004).

Fourth Landmark

Fear

I am losing all hope; I am paralyzed with fear.... Come
quickly, Lord, and answer me, for my depression deepens....
Show me where to walk.... Lead me in good paths, for your
Spirit is good.

PSALM 143:4, 7–8, 10

Fear was one of the major subjects that compelled me to write this guidebook. Fear stops us from being who God is calling us to be. Fear keeps us from doing the things He desires that we do. Fear enters into so many of our decisions, both important and trivial.

Fear is defined as "an instinctive emotion aroused by impending or seeming danger, pain, or evil." Its God-given function is to sense a destructive force or situation and impel us to defensive action. This type of momentary fear is useful and infrequent, often combined with a rush of adrenaline to help us escape harm.

However, as I discussed in the last chapter, when we stop trusting our instincts, we place ourselves in harm's way. In the context of our husband's betrayal, the things we should fear and respond to, we ignore—to our detriment—when, in fact, we should approach them with freedom. When we consistently operate out of fear, the benefits of adrenaline are lost, and instead it drains our health.

God built us to be in intimate relationship with others. We need emotional intimacy and physical touch to maintain good mental, emotional, and physical health. Women end up physically ill because of weakened immune systems as a result of chronic fear. Living under these self-induced conditions is what the Bible calls having a spirit of fear (see 2 Timothy 1:7). God wants to free you from this destructive condition.

Every person will experience fear from time to time in certain circumstances. Remaining stuck in fear is what becomes the problem. We can experience fear and still retain the courage to do what's right. Fear may be present, but it will take a backseat when you put faith in the driver's seat. We might not grasp the victory of trust in God immediately, but if we consistently practice, peace will prevail. As this next scripture suggests, when fear grips us, we are to look to God for courage and seek out a healthy paradigm for facing our problems.

> When I am afraid, I will put my confidence in you. Yes, I will trust the promises of God. And since I am trusting him, what can mere man do to me? (Psalm 56:3–4)

Putting this verse into practical action is the focus of this chapter.

Behind the Mask

As you may have guessed, I am intimately acquainted with fear. I spent much of my adult life acting out of fear-based thinking, and it was not until I began to go through my own healing process that I realized how much other people act out of fear too. My fear determined my relationships. I maintained a great facade, but I so badly needed to always be in a relationship that my fear of not having a boyfriend led me to be in relationships with men whom I knew were not right. The neediness was there before I started dating at thirteen, but it only became evident to me at that point. I would stay with a relationship, even one I didn't like, until a replacement came along. And it took me many years to learn why.

My faulty thinking looked something like this:
- Independence = Aloneness. Avoid at all cost.
- Man dependence = Intimacy. Obtain at any cost.
- God dependence = Sacrifice. Avoid. You won't get what you want.

You may have operated from a similar set of beliefs, or you may not identify with this at all. But I hope you realize God's heart for you. As Brenda and I point out in *The*

Healing Choice, He wants us to have healthy, intimate relationships—with Him and with others.

Beyond independence and man dependence, there's a middle ground of *interdependence*—the give-and-take of any ideal relationship. Interdependence is how God designed us to relate to one another; it's the mutual ground where intimacy and individuality can coexist. Love, not fear, is the driving force in interdependent relationships.

Incredibly, fear in one's heart is addressed in the Bible more than five hundred times! God knew we would trip ourselves up in this area and sometimes become bound up by fear. That is why His Word keeps telling us to not fear.

> Fear not, for I am with you. Do not be dismayed. I am your God. I will
> strengthen you; I will help you; I will uphold you with my victorious right
> hand. (Isaiah 41:10)

Low self-esteem, remaining stuck in bad situations, living with abuse, panic disorders, obsessive-compulsive behaviors, seeking approval—all of these have one common cause: fear. Your fear may manifest itself in areas other than relationships. But for our purposes in this guidebook, I want you to focus on fear as it pertains to (1) your relationships, and (2) doing God's will.

Consider some of our common thoughts and statements from childhood to adulthood:

- *They might not be friends with me if I don't do it.*
- *They'll think I'm a geek if I wear that, Mom!*
- *He's a jerk, but if we break up, I won't have a date for the prom.*
- *If I don't sleep with him, he'll dump me.*
- *I can't make it on my paycheck alone.*
- *If I give my heart to God, He'll send me to Africa.*
- *What if my biological clock runs out?*
- *It will be better after we're married.*
- *At my age, you can't be so particular.*

Again, all of these have fear as their common origin; specifically, the fear of losing relationship or intimacy. At an even more basic level is the underlying fear that God will not meet our needs. We often fan those fears ourselves too, because few of us really understand just how much God wants to help His children: "I am holding you by your right hand—I, the Lord your God—and I say to you, Don't be afraid; I am here to help you" (Isaiah 41:13).

Most women don't believe they operate out of fear and, when asked, will tell you they are not fearful at all. But if you analyze their negative thoughts and actions, you'll often find fear as a common root. That's not how things ought to be for us as Christians, of course. Contrast what we commonly experience with what we see in the Bible: "There is no fear in love" (1 John 4:18, NIV). Or as The Living Bible puts it: "We need have no fear of someone who loves us perfectly; his perfect love for us eliminates all dread of what he might do to us. If we are afraid, it is for fear of what he might do to us and shows that we are not fully convinced that he really loves us." In other words, where love exists, fear cannot dwell.

This can be a difficult concept. It certainly was for me. To understand it more fully, examine the statement in reverse: When we are operating out of fear, we are not operating out of love. When fear is the deciding or ruling force, it smothers love. Fear smothers doing the loving thing, what is best for the other person. Fear doesn't generate love. It is grasping, selfish, insatiable.

Who wants to admit to all that in herself? This is why fear can be very difficult to see in ourselves. One woman, Carolyn, finally spotted it one day in her own spiritual mirror after prayer:

> As I sought the Lord to forgive my husband for his erratic and hurtful behavior, He turned my focus toward my own heart—and it hasn't been pretty. The past month or so, I've learned how my life has been controlled by my own fear, and that this has created walls between my husband, Tim, and me. This is the very thing that Tim has mentioned to me on and off for years but that I couldn't see in myself before. Tim has very much wanted relationship with me but has felt hopeless in connecting with me because of my fear. This does not justify any of his hurtful actions against me, but by God's grace I've now realized that I've been a big part of the problem too. I need to learn to trust God so that He can give me a new heart and so that He can help me meet Tim's needs, right where he's at.

Carolyn found out what so many of us have also learned all too well—the actions taken in fear create myriad unhealthy responses of their own, the most common of which we'll examine in the next two chapters.

Fear Doesn't Risk

Many of our initial reactions to our husbands' sin are damaging and rooted in fear. We fear that we'll lose the relationship—the security, comfort, and companionship—as well as happiness, social stature, and financial support. We can't immediately see how we can hold it all together if we draw the line on his behavior. We fear the outcome, so we don't risk holding him accountable or standing up for our God and the destiny He has in mind for our family.

We want things to change, but not if change means we might lose it all. We don't trust God enough. We fear instead. Bound by such fear, a woman can't or won't allow God far enough into her situation to do any real good. She will only respond in her own strength and rationalize that she isn't disbelieving God, telling herself, *I'm just taking one day at a time,* or, *I'm just trying to love my husband through.* But in most cases, her heart knows the real truth.

Psychologists say we are attracted to what we're familiar with, and codependent people are addicted to familiar, unhealthy relationships. I agree, and I believe that this is the reason many hurting women avoid change, but for others, there is an entirely different dynamic at play. These women know that the relationships they're stuck in are unhealthy, but they simply fear the unknown. The terrifying question, *Who else will love me?* can be every bit as paralyzing as codependence.

We've all known people stuck in a miserable job they disliked, but the idea of looking for something better frightened them. How many people stay stuck where they are in a miserable marriage and never take a stand with their husbands so they can build something better together? No one knows for sure, but we can all be certain of one thing: fear can easily overwhelm the best of us. The risk involved, the possibility of rejection, or the fear of having no one can cause us to cling to what's tangible, the "bird in the hand," even if that bird is just an ugly vulture, ripping away at the rotting carcass of our marriage.

People do the same thing with a bad restaurant, the same old vacation year after year, an outdated hairstyle. It's more comfortable for us to stick with what's known than to face the unknown. Fear chains us to the comfortable, far away from the scary "what ifs" of life. If fear can chain us to our same old restaurants and hairstyles, how much more can it lock us down in an unhealthy relationship?

The fear of being alone can swallow women whole. For many a woman, the fear of being alone is so great that she'd rather stay with the man abusing her and her children than leave. Her fear is an awful double-edged sword. She's terrified of being alone and yet terrified of him when he is present.

According to God, fear is not part of a healthy relationship, no matter what you've been convinced of otherwise: "Fear of man is a dangerous trap, but to trust in God means safety" (Proverbs 29:25).

Fear is dangerous because it blinds you to where your trust in God is lacking. When red flags start flying even before marriage, a woman afraid of being alone doesn't leave her man, no matter how unfit he may be for her. Instead, she rationalizes or denies his behavior. If she trusted God, she wouldn't need to fear being alone; she wouldn't look at the future through the distorting window of fear. This chart helps us spot other areas where we fear rather than trust.

Fear of...	Manifests as...
• being alone • needs being unmet • rejection • taking care of self	neediness and insecurity
• others seeing imperfections • others knowing my past • exposure of his actions • dependence • intimacy	shame and isolation

Notice how the list begins with fear of being alone and ends with fear of intimacy. Yet the truth is, these fears can also often be found together. We can be needy and isolated emotionally even when we are with people all the time. This creates a difficult conflict, because the desire to connect does not always mean that we want to be known intimately. It may simply mean that we fear rejection.

Lord, when doubts fill my mind, when my heart is in turmoil, quiet me and give me renewed hope and cheer. (Psalm 94:19)

Panic and Paralysis

When I am speaking to a woman about the need to consider new boundaries with her husband, I sometimes suggest praying to God about His thoughts on a temporary separation from the marriage. The singular, most common response from a passive woman is *the look,* that deer-in-the-headlights panic or momentary paralysis, which often leads immediately to a rushing cascade of reasons why she couldn't possibly separate from him. And I never even said she should separate! I simply suggested she pray about it.

Do you see how she decided to leave God out of the equation? Why? She's afraid He'll ask her to trust Him and do something terrifyingly risky, so she instead chooses to make up her mind without Him, even though her thinking isn't clear and her thoughts are clouded by fear. Yet "God has not given us a spirit of fear, but of power and of love and of a sound mind" (2 Timothy 1:7, NKJV).

When a wife rejects even the idea of praying about a temporary boundary of separation, she may be expressing one or more of these common reasons:

- *But then I'd be alone.*
- *I don't want to end up divorced.*
- *I'm afraid of not being able to care for my children and myself financially.*
- *He'll be too angry if I tell him to leave.*
- *He'll act out even more if we separate.*
- *I could never find another husband.*
- *How will I know if he's changing if we're not together?*

A woman operating from fear-based thinking handicaps her ability to listen to God. She tends to fast-forward into a future that holds her worst-fear conclusions and make her decisions based on those conclusions. That thinking sends her down a destructive path in alternating states of panic and paralysis.

> For you closed your eyes to the facts and did not choose to reverence and trust the Lord, and you turned your back on me, spurning my advice. That is why you must eat the bitter fruit of having your own way, and experience the full terrors of the pathway you have chosen. For you turned away from me—to death; your own complacency will kill you. Fools! But all who listen to me shall live in peace and safety, unafraid. (Proverbs 1:29–33)

"I've Got Everything Under Control"

If I can control his activities, his time, and his environment, he won't act out.
If I take care of all the responsibilities, he won't have any reason to act out.
A woman's fear of her husband's acting out (or even leaving her) may be manifested in an attempt to control him and the world around him. She may try controlling by "pleasing" him, engaging in immoral activities to keep his behaviors at home. If you recognize this need to control in yourself, I tell you plainly that this approach will never work to contain, placate, or satisfy him. His lust knows no limits. You're not capable of filling this thirst. In fact, no human is.

This is because a man's compromises are born of his own wounds and his own choices, and his sexual sin is his medication of choice. It's not about you, and it never has been about you. The only appropriate fear in your situation is a reverent fear of God. For some, fearing God brings to mind a picture of a brutal father, one who is remembered from childhood.

But you are His daughter. When you know God's real nature, His power matched with limitless love, you will discover a fear born of respect and adoration. You'll want to listen to Him, and you'll lose the desire to cower in a corner. If this is you, God wants to renew your mind and teach you about Himself—as He truly is—a loving, passionate, and fully involved Father. He wants you to trust Him.

MY · STONE · WORK

Insight

Go back through your life, and write down the fear-based decisions you made. Note areas where you repeated mistakes. Was fear to blame? Then analyze your current situation, and journal about areas in which you may be struggling with fear today. Where is fear getting in the way of receiving God's wisdom?

Explore the beliefs that need to change in order for you to eliminate fear and stop it from controlling your behavior.

Action

To be free from fear, you must make moment-by-moment decisions to speak God's truth into your circumstances. You'll find extensive, practical instruction on how to do this in our book, *The Healing Choice*. You will also need to recognize that the torment of fear comes from the great tormentor, God's Enemy. That is why Scripture will be absolutely crucial to you in this battle. Using a Bible concordance, find your favorite references on fear (you can also search the term at IBS.org). Select several that speak to you, and write them in your journal and on a small card to carry with you.

Each time you find yourself reacting out of fear, speak out your chosen scriptures. Write in your journal, below the current fearful thoughts, how you are going to respond in God's wisdom to the circumstance and how you plan to reject fearful responses. Finally, establish accountability with your walking companion to listen to your fears and help you find clarity in your thoughts.

My Prayer to Overcome Fear

Lord, sometimes my fear so overwhelms me, I feel like a frightened child inside. I'm afraid of being alone, yet I'm afraid of living dependent on anyone. I'm afraid of being hurt again, but I grow heavy in trying to protect my heart; sometimes I fear it is turning to stone. I fear for my children. I fear for my future. But You know all this and more about my troubled mind and heart. Lord, give me the courage to do the right thing, even if that means I stand alone. I know You are standing with me. Lord, strengthen me; bring Your promises to life in my soul! Renew my trust in You. In Jesus Christ's name, I pray, amen.

Further Resources

On fear: *Living Fearlessly,* Sheila Walsh (Grand Rapids: Zondervan, 2001).

On understanding God as Father: *Tactics,* Fred Stoeker (Colorado Springs: Water-Brook, 2006).

On learning how to trust God: *The Healing Choice,* Brenda Stoeker and Susan Allen (Colorado Springs: WaterBrook, 2008).

Fifth Landmark

Passive Responses

The Lord is good and glad to teach the proper path to all
who go astray; he will teach the ways that are right and
best to those who humbly turn to him. And when we
obey him, every path he guides us on is fragrant with his
lovingkindness and his truth.

PSALM 25:8–10

When a woman fears her husband may be deceiving her, her first responses might include some unhealthy ways to deal with the situation. Some of the common unhealthy responses look like this:

- insisting on getting to the bottom of it immediately
- confronting him with some newly discovered evidence
- believing his explanations and excuses, despite clear facts
- bouncing between believing what she intuitively knows is the truth and his weak explanations that she wants to believe
- doing things that are contrary to her own morals and better judgment in an effort to hold her marriage together
- pretending to the world that everything is okay in her household
- repeating responses one through six in a vicious cycle of desperation

This scenario illustrates both passive and assertive means of dealing with deception. Also, it will not apply to all of us, since every woman is unique in personality and in her response to suspicious behavior. Nevertheless, this chapter and the next will help you to understand your own responses and identify any unhealthy reactions you may have already had when faced with a crisis in your marriage. This chapter focuses on responses that dumb down what you know, or "go along to get along." To put an image to the idea, picture yourself trying to drive a car that's stuck in neutral—you aren't connecting things, so you shouldn't assume that anything is going to happen.

If you have had no training for this experience (and who has?), or if unhealthy responses were modeled in your family of origin as the "coping mechanisms of choice," it is very probable that you have resorted to counterproductive reactions to fix the problems with your husband.

MY • STONE • WORK

Insight

Read the following list and note those items you identify with.

Complicity
- presented a united front of marital harmony to family, friends, and church
- kept secrets to protect husband
- lied to cover up for husband

Denial
- denied personal intuitions
- kept busy and overextended to avoid reality
- found evidence of deceit but didn't respond to it

Loss of Self
- gave up life goals, hobbies, interests, or friends
- acted against own morals, values, and beliefs

- changed dress or appearance to accommodate husband
- accepted husband's sexual norms as own
- stopped going on outings/trips that would leave husband unsupervised
- stopped taking care of personal needs and appearance
- made a subconscious bargain with self to ignore his behavior to preserve the marriage/lifestyle
- developed your own addiction

Passivity

- was not willing to take action or enforce consequences when it was the right thing to do
- stopped discussing family, personal, and household issues with husband so as not to trigger a mood swing
- used his problems as an excuse for your own
- spiritualized the problem; only prayed but took no action
- saw yourself as a perpetual victim of his actions

If you recognized yourself frequently in the lists, you are by no means alone. But I've noticed that women respond to this list in a variety of ways. Many immediately realize how futile some of their responses have been and make changes to deal with the problem in new, more productive ways. Others resist change, refusing to believe their actions are not godly, and still others fall somewhere in between, understanding that their responses aren't having the desired effect but struggling with whether their actions are truly poor alternatives to more effective, godly responses.

There is no vacillation in the medical/psychiatric model of the listed responses, however. This set of unhealthy responses is called a disease, and the model goes so far as to give this disease a name. It is called codependency, and the person exhibiting the symptoms—those listed above—is labeled an enabler. Both are modern-day terminologies for very old responses. Of course, God identified the root causes long ago: humans groping for solutions to their problems by using their own meager reasoning powers alone. The biblical model of codependency is simply humans in their natural fallen state—*outside of dependency on God.*

What does our reasoning look like apart from God's intervention? Comprised of unhealthy emotions or incorrect thinking, our human reasoning leads to these unhealthy responses: fear/worry, shame, self-blame, denial, neediness, control, lack of wisdom, pride, greed, manipulation, and helplessness.

Of course, as humans created in God's image, we can choose to rise above this kind of human reasoning, as this woman did:

> A few months ago I resolved to not be codependent in this matter of my
> husband's addiction, like questioning him constantly, worrying about what
> he's thinking about during sex or worrying about what he's doing when
> a gorgeous woman walks into view. It was driving me insane. I decided I
> would leave it up to my husband and the Lord, because ultimately it is my
> husband's deal, and he is solely responsible and accountable for his thoughts
> and actions.

If we, too, are driving ourselves insane by our own thoughts yet won't shift gears to change course, why the resistance? The answer is simple but deceptively complex: *we become overdependent on relationships when we don't have a dependent relationship with God.* We must fear and trust Him above all others.

Even the Jewish leaders had trouble separating their dependence on God from dependence on others. Most Christians are sure they wouldn't have made the same mistake the Jewish leaders did. But we are each guilty of their compromise in some ways:

> However, even many of the Jewish leaders believed him to be the Messiah but
> wouldn't admit it to anyone because of their fear that the Pharisees would excom-
> municate them from the synagogue; for they loved the praise of men more than
> the praise of God.
>
> Jesus shouted to the crowds, "If you trust me, you are really trusting God."
> (John 12:42–44)

The First Lie in Paradise

It is widely accepted that codependents and addicts adopt these coping mechanisms because of abuse and abandonment in childhood. Stopping the pain and filling the void with something or someone they can control seems to be the wounded one's greatest need.

Yet while these childhood factors do indeed inflict deep wounds, they simply cannot explain the whole puzzle. For instance, let's look at Adam and Eve. They had perfect parenting. They lived in Paradise. They had everything they needed. Yet something was amiss. Why was the serpent's suggestion too tempting to refuse? Apparently he got to the vulnerable part of the heart of humankind. How? He approached them using man's own reasoning as described in Genesis 3, New International Version.

The serpent said, "You will not surely die" (verse 4). Eve decided to believe the snake and distrust God. She exhibited lack of wisdom in disbelieving God's truth, which led her to be easily deceived. The serpent said, "For God knows that when you eat of it your eyes will be opened" (verse 5). When Eve stopped trusting God, she wanted to have information to control her fate. There was a sense of God's withholding something good, and intellectual greed crept in. When the serpent said, "And you will be like God, knowing good and evil" (verse 5), Eve's desire for power became a driving force; she believed that she could be self-guided and have access to all knowledge on the same level as God. She would no longer need God.

Once Eve was deceived, she felt compelled to convince Adam of the same beliefs. The serpent was finished with his work for the time being, because Eve was enthusiastically doing his job for him. She manipulated her husband to join her in disobedience. After they had both indulged and she realized the plan had fallen apart, they both continued acting from their own distorted reasoning. Genesis 3 continues:

Adam and Eve: they sewed fig leaves together, they both felt shame in being vulnerable before each other, and intimacy took three steps backward.

The LORD: "Where are you?" (verse 9). Of course, God knew.

Adam: "I heard you in the garden, and I was afraid because I was naked; so I hid" (verse 10). Adam expressed fear and shame toward God, whereas before there was only childlike trust and innocence. Intimacy with God just took a giant leap backward.

Adam: "The woman you put here with me—she gave me some fruit from the tree, and I ate it" (verse 12). Neither Adam nor Eve took responsibility for their actions.

Eve: "The serpent deceived me, and I ate" (verse 13). They both blamed others. They both played the victim.

In this one event, Adam and Eve displayed many of the same unhealthy responses listed earlier. As so often happens with us, they were enticed into thinking they could set up a life that would be dependent on something they could control. That seemed a better bet than depending on God, whom they couldn't control. Their story illustrates a root cause of unhealthy responses: mistrust of God.

I will address other root causes in depth in later chapters. For now, let's look at why our unhealthy responses do not deliver the desired results.

Complicity

Keeping up a happy facade to disguise a troubled marriage involves lying. It keeps evil hidden in a dark place, where it continues to thrive. Of course, God does not want us to lie; He wants us to shed His light on evil. Thus, unveiling evil is the first step toward being able to bring His power into the midst of it. Unveiling evil to bring truth means bringing together other people who may be able to help and pray for you both, despite the discomfort of the less-than-perfect circumstances you may currently share. Bringing evil to light also commands hidden shame to lose its grip and frees up energy to work on new solutions.

> Laughter cannot mask a heavy heart. When the laughter ends, the grief remains. (Proverbs 14:13)

In bringing your situation to light, you do not need to hang up banners revealing every ugly truth to the world. You do not need to tell the grocery checker how you're really feeling. You do need to thoughtfully, prayerfully, and with discernment determine to tell the people who are closest to you what has been going on. These would be leaders, friends, and family members who will be able to stand with you, guide you, and be understanding without shaming either one of you. Ideally, they are people who love you and your husband enough that they would be willing to invest their time in you. Pray and ask the Lord to show you which people in your life right now would offer this kind of help and support.

Denial

We explored denial in the chapter dealing with emotions of loss. So I will simply emphasize here the importance of moving beyond the initial response of denial that may arrive involuntarily. Simply put, if we deny to ourselves, and others, that there is a problem, we sidestep any responsibility to deal with it. Living with the status quo, as painful as it is, may seem easier than the alternative—at least for a while.

Women who have determined to keep their marriages at any cost frequently use denial as their chief strategy to get through life. These are the women who intentionally remain unconscious of reality. They don't want to see the truth. They don't want to know what is really happening.

Be willing to see the truth. If you want to have any real chance of saving your marriage, you must take off the blinders. Why? Denial precludes any possibility of change and usually enables the problem to get worse. Denial will only lead to further decay of the home you are neglecting to acknowledge needs repair!

The wise man looks ahead. The fool attempts to fool himself and won't face facts. (Proverbs 14:8)

Loss of Self

When a serious loss is occurring, a woman may not even realize what is happening to her. She may not be aware of the slow erosion of her personality, her appearance, her interests, and her morals. Day by day, a wife may unconsciously give up more and more of her own legitimate needs in order to be more "available" to her husband.

What she may not be admitting to herself is that the real reason she stopped taking her art class on Wednesday nights is that she could not attend it and still be able to keep tabs on her husband's whereabouts during that time period. Know that this approach has never stopped an unfaithful one from getting what he wants. He will find a time to do his thing whether or not his wife makes it difficult. Withdrawing from her own interests won't solve the problem; instead it creates more damage in her life as it leads to isolation.

Some women find themselves dressing in certain ways and having sexual encounters with their husbands that are degrading to them in an attempt to "fill" their husbands' desires, so they will not need to act out elsewhere. I have known women who attempt to keep their husbands "home" by this method, but the price they pay is great. Their husbands are no less addicted. Their desire is not for their wives, who are nothing more than actresses playing a role in the husbands' ongoing fantasies. They are not experiencing intimacy. The husbands remain focused entirely upon the intensity of the experience. Nothing has changed.

Except for the changes in the wife, that is. The demand placed on a wife by her husband's increasing appetite eventually causes her to despise herself, to be prone to depression, and to live in shame. She exposes herself to all the pornography that he wants to bring home and enters into the sin with him.

> My [daughter], if sinners entice you, do not consent. (Proverbs 1:10, NKJV)

> If a godly [woman] compromises with the wicked, it is like polluting a fountain
> or muddying a spring. (Proverbs 25:26)

Passivity

It has been wisely noted that in order for much of the evil to persist in this world, good people need simply do nothing. Bury your head, sit on the fence, complain, and do absolutely nothing. But God strongly opposes this kind of lukewarm, actionless response to wrongdoing.

> I know your deeds, that you are neither cold nor hot. I wish you were either one
> or the other! So, because you are lukewarm—neither hot nor cold—I am about
> to spit you out of my mouth.... To him who overcomes, I will give the right to
> sit with me on my throne, just as I overcame and sat down with my Father on his
> throne. (Revelation 3:15–16, 21, NIV)

Though it may appear saintly, passivity is one of the Enemy's greatest weapons, which he uses to keep us paralyzed, unable to deal with evil. We were never meant to stand by passively, allowing evil to prosper. Instead, we are to ask God for wisdom and courage for His means to confront and overcome it.

Passivity is often confused with peace. The truth is, you can be in the middle of a war and be at peace, knowing you are doing the right thing. Peace will not come by wishing away the things that threaten your life. Peace will come when your thoughts and actions are in sync with God's.

At some point you have to stop crying to God to change things and, instead, take the action that God has already told you to take. Even Moses had to be reminded of this as he stood at the shore facing the Red Sea:

> But Moses told the people, "Don't be afraid. Just stand where you are and watch, and you will see the wonderful way the Lord will rescue you today. The Egyptians you are looking at—you will never see them again. The Lord will fight for you, and you won't need to lift a finger!"
>
> Then the Lord said to Moses, "Quit praying and get the people moving! Forward, march! Use your rod—hold it out over the water, and the sea will open up a path before you, and all the people of Israel shall walk through on dry ground! (Exodus 14:13–16)

When God asks us to do something, it may seem like an impossible mission viewed through our human logic. That is where faith enters in. If God is calling you to an action, He will make a way for you. He is pleased when you exercise your faith, as Paul writes:

> You need to keep on patiently doing God's will if you want him to do for you all that he has promised.... And those whose faith has made them good in God's sight must live by faith, trusting him in everything. Otherwise, if they shrink back, God will have no pleasure in them. (Hebrews 10:36, 38)

We can be outwardly passive yet inwardly brewing many sinful thoughts. Many women, when trying to see a way to end their husbands' behavior, have thoughts they are ashamed to admit. It often goes something like this: He is very late coming home. She dreads what he may be doing. She hopes he has been in a fatal car accident. That would be a relief, she thinks, rather than to find out he has been at it again. Some women go a little further and entertain fantasies about taking measures into their own hands to put an end to their husbands' lives and to their own misery. These kinds of thoughts stem from a sense of helplessness, because we feel like an eternal victim if we stand by passively, hoping for them to change. Yet, "If I had cherished sin in my heart, the Lord would not have listened" (Psalm 66:18, NIV).

Some of us came into marriage with passive rules defining how to live—learned from our own first families—and the destructive behaviors we were instructed to overlook. These rules may never have been voiced, but they were modeled in the behavior of those in authority. Echoing deep in our subconscious minds, they tell us:

- *Don't respond to evil.*
- *Protect the evildoer.*
- *Don't talk to outsiders.*
- *Don't stand up for yourself.*

We have learned that we must be passive at any cost. This is the "nice-girl syndrome," which in reality is not nice at all and certainly isn't Christian. You can't be a passive "nice girl" and a good helpmate to your husband at the same time:

Your job [as his helpmate] is to help him see and open his heart and ears to God.

Men are slower at understanding relationships, and we can't forget that our husbands have blind spots that result from their [sexual] hardwiring. Your goal is to speed up his learning curve by grinding with the iron and pointing out clearly what God means by being trustworthy.

Confront him. Be excruciatingly honest about your pain. Remove the wiggle room with the precision of a surgeon, talking straight about how he is failing you and how you are losing respect for him.

At the same time, don't retaliate, don't manipulate, and don't play games. You're not here to hurt him but to help him. You're not fighting for your way but to have things God's way....

You do it by defending God's boundaries and not your own. Be transparent, persistent, and resolute....

You aren't there to attack the man—you are here to boost the man. It's not your ministry to bring him back to you sexually. It's your ministry to bring him back to God spiritually. It may be hard to keep this as your focus, but it's the right focus. (*Every Heart Restored*, 190–91)

Strength like this brings true peace to your relationship. The passive, nice-girl syndrome only contributes to our feeling that we will forever be victims of others' bad behavior because we don't know any nice way to make them stop mistreating us. And if we do manage to implement boundaries and consequences for another's destructive actions, we end up feeling undeserved guilt, because our consciences have been trained to both hide from and be numb to sin. We need to "stop listening to teaching that contradicts what you know is right" (Proverbs 19:27).

In the next chapter, we'll look at unhealthy, counterproductive reactions. For now, consider what areas of your life might benefit from stronger boundaries. The first logical place to put boundaries in place is in the area of sex. If you do not trust your husband, the only healthy stand is to tell him clearly that you are unwilling to compromise yourself sexually because you don't know if he is still engaging in risky behaviors.

A wife who pretends everything is okay is deceitful. She perpetuates his delusion that his behavior is not affecting the marriage. Similarly, hiding from him or perpetually "having a headache" is equally unproductive: it avoids speaking the truth about why you are unwilling to be sexual with him.

Winking at sin leads to sorrow; bold reproof leads to peace. (Proverbs 10:10)

MY • STONE • WORK

Insight

Take inventory of your situation as you review the list of passive stances at the beginning of this landmark, and consider in what ways you have been avoiding conflict by adopting a passive stance. Journal your insights, and add to the list as you become aware of other areas of passivity.

Action

We must throw out the old rule book! We need to replace it with God's rule book. The Bible needs to be our daily reference for finding out how to live, how to respond, and how to take action. The book of Proverbs is a great book of the Bible to read daily. It is referred to as one of the wisdom books. I love Proverbs because the proverbs get right to the heart of the matter, the bottom line. In a single sentence, a proverb takes a principle down to its essence.

You must throw away your image of being a "good girl" and grow up into a strong godly woman, even if that doesn't seem to come naturally to you.

Each time you find yourself passively coping with a stressful situation, stop! This is a great time to ask God how to respond. It's also a great time to call your walking companion to hold you accountable—to encourage you to seek an appropriate response to your circumstances.

· · · · · · · · · · · · · · ❁ · · · · · · · · · · · · ·

Prayer for My Passive Responses

Change my heart, God, to desire Your wisdom and understanding. Change my heart, God, to desire You more than anything this world has to offer. Change my heart, God, to desire pleasing You more than pleasing any man. Change my heart, God, to desire to be more like You in all things. In Jesus Christ's name, amen.

· ·

Further Resources
Love Must Be Tough, James C. Dobson (Dallas: Word, 1983).

Sixth Landmark

Counterproductive Reactions

You have turned from the God who can save you—the
Rock who can hide you; therefore, even though you plant
a wonderful, rare crop of greatest value...your only harvest
will be a pile of grief and incurable pain.

ISAIAH 17:10–11

Continuing our discussion of responses to betrayal, the focus here is on more aggressive reactions. Though they are more active, they're actually counterproductive to healing the hurt and helping the marriage.

MY · STONE · WORK

Insight

Review the list below and see if you've been having any counterproductive reactions to your husband's behavior.

Obsessive Preoccupation

- checked husband's mail, briefcase, pockets, and wallet
- followed husband; drove by places he's known to frequent
- thought constantly about husband's behaviors and motives

Blame and Punishment

- became increasingly more self-righteous and punitive
- was destructive to others
- had affairs to punish your husband

Manipulation

- played the martyr, heroine, or victim role
- used sex to manipulate or patch up disagreements
- made threats to leave but never followed through

Excessive Responsibility

- blamed yourself; believed that if you changed, husband would stop
- took responsibility for husband's behavior
- created situations where you were indispensable

Emotional Turmoil

- emotions were out of control at times
- children and co-workers became targets of anger
- experienced free-floating shame, anxiety, and depression
- always had a crisis or problem
- panicked when husband had unaccountable free time

Did you find yourself in this category more than in the previous passive role? Though a woman doing some of these things may feel like she is putting in effort to deal with the issues, it is effort spent without reward. Let's look at why these reactions don't get the desired results.

Obsessive Preoccupation

The focus of obsessive preoccupation seems to be to get to the truth. At first blush, that sounds like a good thing. However, how you acquire that truth, and what you do with it once you have it, are of paramount importance.

In the process of seeking the truth, a woman may fall into the trap of spending much of her available mental energy trying to discover what her husband is up to. There is often an adrenaline rush that accompanies every pocket search or surreptitious drive-by.

Then there is the evidence itself. Most women have, at different times, come across things they question: mysterious calls on a phone bill, a receipt, a name and phone number scribbled on a scrap of paper or matchbook. These pieces of evidence naturally trigger an alarm in your mind. You analyze the possibilities, all the while getting sick to your stomach. You confront your husband with it, and he explains it away as nothing as you put him through interrogation—desperately hoping he'll tell the truth.

Unable to build a strong case, you eventually dismiss the evidence and tell yourself, *Well, it certainly was not enough to convict him in court. Guess I was wrong.* The problem is, however, that you are left with nagging doubts. The receipt may have uncovered a discrepancy between where he was at a given time and where he was supposed to be; in other words, he lied to you. Though your brain is working overtime trying to buy your husband's explanation, your mind cannot put the evidence to rest. So you are back on his trail to find new evidence, something irrefutable, ironclad.

The trouble is, though, that most of what you'll deem to be evidence will be no more than circumstantial. Since catching your husband red-faced and red-handed is not very probable, you'll forever feel short on evidence, compelled to search for one more thing to cap your case. Furthermore, the part of you that does not want to believe this ugly truth about your husband will work against you, refusing to let you take action until you are 100 percent sure of the crime. Yet another part of you lives with the persistent hope that, with just a little pressure, the truth will finally burst forth as your husband confesses, his conscience finally winning out over evil. So you search incessantly for ways to apply that pressure.

How does one uncover the truth without resorting to such craziness? Once you feel you know the truth, what should you do with it? God does want to reveal truth to you, but He doesn't want you ruled by obsessive anxiety. Simply ask God to uncover the truth that you need to see and to grant you the courage to respond to the truth with wisdom. He will give you peace as you trust Him to bring your husband's sin out of hiding, and that will free your mind to focus on thoughts that bring health and life to your body.

> Don't worry about anything; instead, pray about everything; tell God your needs and don't forget to thank him for his answers. If you do this you will experience God's peace, which is far more wonderful than the human mind can understand. His peace will keep your thoughts and your hearts quiet and at rest as you trust in Christ Jesus. (Philippians 4:6–7)

As you ask the Holy Spirit to reveal important evidence to you, He will—and in very practical ways. He'll show you the types of evidence you've been seeking, but you will not have been obsessing about it, wasting your life in pursuit of it. I have heard countless stories of women who, while cleaning the garage, came across a pile of pornography or, while packing a suitcase, found a slip of paper with a strange phone number on it. Some were doing their bills or emptying a waste can when they found something that was clear evidence of deceit. These women literally stumbled on the information; they had not drained their energies day after day searching for it. "When the Holy Spirit, who is truth, comes, he shall guide you into all truth, for he will not be presenting his own ideas, but will be passing on to you what he has heard" (John 16:13).

I have heard stories of women being prompted by the Holy Spirit to call their husbands, go home early, or surprise them at work. Others, being awakened from sleep, felt impressed to walk into their husbands' study. Here's one woman's story:

> I woke up this morning earlier than I ever do. I don't know why, but I just woke up. I had a strong feeling that I should go to the bathroom...so I did. I then had

a very strong and clear thought, which I believe came from God, to look under the bathroom rug. I thought, *Look under the bathroom rug?* I never do that. My husband of three and a half years was already awake and in the shower, only a few feet from where I was standing, but I looked under the rug anyway and found a magazine.

It wasn't pornography—it was a men's and women's clothing catalog that we got in the mail and that I had already thrown away. At first the catalog seemed fairly innocent, but it did have four pages showing women modeling underwear and bras and a few other pretty revealing pictures of women, thoughtfully clothed. Somehow, I knew what had just happened.

I didn't know what to do, so I just put the magazine back under the rug, went back to the bedroom, and waited for my husband to get out of the shower. When he came into the room and saw that I was awake, he joined me in bed. I asked him if he had anything he wanted to tell me, deciding to approach him with a question, rather than accusing him.

"Like what?" he said.

"Just wondering if you felt like you needed to tell me something," I replied calmly.

"Uhh…maybe," he said a bit nervously.

"Okay, what is it?" I asked.

He confessed that he had just masturbated in the bathroom. I told him I already knew and that, strangely enough, it was God who had led me to find out.

In all cases where wives uncovered a deceit with the help of the Holy Spirit, they were immediately ready to take the next step of confronting their husbands, even if they didn't have an open-and-shut case. All they needed was to recognize that some element of trust in the relationship was violated. The evidence was clear enough. When intuition sounds the alarm, proceed with caution and pray, trusting God's direction as you go.

Another element of obsessive preoccupation concerns information you may already have. At this point, perhaps you're well aware of betrayal committed by your husband. Often a woman will review this information over and over in her mind. It plays like a tape in her head. She will live in torment as she recounts what he did. If she doesn't have a lot of details, she fills them in with her imagination, usually to her own disadvantage.

Sometimes the memories play involuntarily as something triggers a thought. Sometimes she puts on the tape with intent. Why would a woman put herself through this? Maybe to search for a clue as to why it happened. Maybe to become wary or to protect herself from its happening again. Possibly the Enemy is tormenting her. Whatever the reason, playing the betrayal tape brings no answers—and no relief either! It only brings despair, depression, and fresh pain.

MY · STONE · WORK

Insight

Take inventory of the behaviors you've been obsessively doing. Write your list in your journal. Add to it as you become aware of any other counterproductive reactions.

God does want to reveal truth to you. He also knows if you are willing to respond to the truth in His way. Are you prepared to face reality and to follow God's Word and His promptings? Ask God to prepare your heart to face painful realities His way.

Consider this: What did you do with information you're already aware of? What consequences and boundaries did you put into place? Decide if there is some godly action you need to take.

Action

So the memories are there. While there's no such thing as a memory eraser, you don't need to dwell on the offenses committed against you. This isn't about denial. It's about controlling what you allow your mind to be saturated with. Even when thoughts come involuntarily, we must make a conscious choice to refuse to let them remain our focus. If this sounds like your struggle, there is a scripture just for you. When you find yourself obsessing, turn to this:

Though we live in the world, we do not wage war as the world does. The weapons we fight with are not the weapons of the world. On the contrary, they have divine power to demolish strongholds. We demolish arguments and every pretension that sets itself up against the knowledge of God, and we take captive every thought to make it obedient to Christ. (2 Corinthians 10:3–5, NIV)

When our hearts' desire is to obey Christ, He supplies us with the power and the wisdom to capture rebel thoughts that would render us ineffective in our actions. He will help us make sense of the senseless devastation in our lives. This following scripture is an instruction for then making our minds available to what God wants to show us.

Call to me and I will answer you and tell you great and unsearchable things you do not know. (Jeremiah 33:3, NIV)

Blame and Punishment

Instead of blaming her husband, a wife may blame her husband's behavior on the person he is involved with. In this way, she is able to put her emotional energy into hunting down and attacking the "real culprit."

I have known women who, in order to punish their husbands, had affairs to get even. Both responses drag women into their own sin in their thoughts and actions. In the end, nothing is accomplished toward dealing with the real problem.

Don't be conceited, sure of your own wisdom. Instead, trust and reverence the Lord, and turn your back on evil; when you do that, then you will be given renewed health and vitality. (Proverbs 3:7–8)

A man's conscience is the Lord's searchlight exposing his hidden motives. (Proverbs 20:27)

Manipulation

Manipulation is simply an attempt to control an outcome. It's like holding a person on puppet strings, thinking, *If I tug this way, I can get him to do this. If I say this, he will do that.* How well has it been working so far? It didn't for me either.

But *refusing* to manipulate worked wonders for Brenda, my coauthor on *The Healing Choice,* in dealing with her husband, Fred:

> Manipulation was not in [Brenda's] arsenal…and its absence did more than any single thing to soften my heart to her help. If I'd reach out after a fight to touch her, she wouldn't pull away. If I'd stomp downstairs in manipulative fury, she'd calmly wait up until I snuck back upstairs. She wouldn't play my games, and she wouldn't start her own.
>
> That doesn't mean her stinging rebukes never hurt, of course. In fact, they always did. Like any guy, I hated to be called out on my character flaws, and she was always dead-on right, much to my private consternation. I often struck back like a wounded rattler.
>
> But unlike my sorry tactics, she never belittled or demeaned me, and she never attacked me personally. Her words were meant to switch on a light in my mind, not shoot a flaming arrow through my head. Though she often stung me, she never wounded me further.
>
> I asked her about her approach one time, and she said, "My reactions to you are always a choice, and when I can't love you for your sake because you are being so harsh, I can always find a way to love you for Jesus's sake because of what He's done for me."
>
> So she hugged me because she loved Jesus, and when she couldn't summon any love and grace for me, she'd forgive me because of what Christ meant to both of us. She was so disciplined in that! She was not out to hurt me or to have her own way. She was out to help me and to have things God's way, normal and true.
> (*Every Heart Restored,* 161–62)

This is a much healthier response than trying to control through manipulation. Besides, when it comes to people and life, there is a limit to what things are actually within our control. Manipulation is a poor substitute for allowing another person to experience natural consequences, which Brenda was allowing Fred to do.

In truth, manipulation can also be a form of avoiding responsible action in our own lives. If someone will just respond to our manipulation (and we may want only good things for him), then we will not have to take any action ourselves to help those natural consequences have their effect and to set boundaries that may be hard to enforce.

If you find yourself using manipulation regularly, you can be fairly sure that your practice in setting logical boundaries and allowing natural consequences is pretty rusty. In this context of a husband's sexual sin, the most often-used form of manipulation is to threaten divorce or separation if he does it "one more time." When you don't follow through on your threat after the next violation, you are no longer taken seriously, like the boy who cried wolf. It is foolish to threaten that which you are not willing to do. It renders the threat ineffective, and you are merely training your husband to not believe what you say. Besides that, what if your husband responds, "Then leave if you don't like it here"? When your manipulation backfires like this, you're left powerless and even more wounded.

The man who sets a trap for others will get caught in it himself. Roll a boulder down on someone, and it will roll back and crush you. (Proverbs 26:27)

Excessive Responsibility

A wife can experience a temporary sense of control by taking the blame for a husband's bad behavior. That's because, if you are to blame, it follows that by doing this or that, you can fix it. It is in your control, right? The only problem is this: it's not true! Unfortunately, a husband will often help you along in this erroneous thinking pattern with statements such as, "If you were only thinner, a little sexier, or better in bed, if only we had sex more often, or if you dressed this way, I wouldn't have this problem."

This kind of thinking is plain wrong. It's extremely likely your husband started sinning sexually long before he even met you. Lust and love are polar opposites: one is taking, the other is giving. For it to be your fault, you would have had to force your husband to objectify people and use them for his own pleasure against his will. It can't be your fault. It doesn't make logical sense on any level.

And yet, if you were a scapegoat for your parents' problems, you may have been set up for this "overfunctioning" behavior as a child. Others may have blamed you for things that were truly not your fault. But if things that went wrong were, in your mind, your fault, then all you had to do was be a good girl and your parents would love each other, Mommy wouldn't drink, Daddy wouldn't have to beat you. Even now, when your efforts to please don't get the desired results, you try harder and become confused because you were told that you had the power to make the other person's problems go away. It never occurs to you that self-control is something another person chooses—independent of any action by you.

> There is living truth in what a good man says, but the mouth of the evil
> man is filled with curses. (Proverbs 10:11)

It is appropriate to examine yourself to see if you bear any justifiable responsibility. However, you should view this examination from God's perspective. If there is a list of accusations coming against you from your husband, review the list carefully and prayerfully, asking which things are valid and which your husband may be using as an excuse for his own bad behavior. People who are sinning are quick to blame another for their actions. It takes no training. Because none of us is perfect, accusations slung at us can sting, especially when there's a shred of truth to them. If you take the bait, you may start believing your husband's problems are your fault. Therefore, you need to discern whether you have consistently let your husband down in a particular area or whether it is only on rare occasions that you have failed to meet the needs you are called to fulfill as his wife.

Another form of accepting excessive responsibility involves taking control of all household, money, and family matters. Subconsciously, a woman who does this assumes her husband depends on her so much he could never want to leave. Yet what often happens is that the irresponsible husband gladly allows his wife to take care of everything and give him more time for selfish pursuits. The only rub that comes for him is when he bumps up against the well-orchestrated system and it stifles his own plans. Then he calls her controlling! This sort of behavior doesn't make a woman indispensable; it makes her easy to control, keep distracted, and take advantage of on a long-term basis.

There is a way that seems right to a man, but in the end it leads to death.
(Proverbs 14:12, NIV)

MY · STONE · WORK

Insight

When you honestly examine your heart before God, you will know if there is a change He wants you to make. He does not shame or condemn you but helps you to make the change.

    The unfortunate truth is that you may, out of necessity or because of your husband's neglect, need to take control of most household matters. Simply examine your motive. Am I doing this out of need—to care for my children and myself—or am I trying to be superwoman to establish my worth?

Action

Work on making the changes that God is showing you are necessary, accepting the possibility that changing yourself may not change a thing in your husband's behavior. Making this effort will, however, free you from condemnation and allow you to order your life without undue guilt and shame over your husband's poor choices.

Emotional Turmoil

Here are several ways in which a woman might allow her emotions to rule her:

- If she always has a crisis brewing, she can give her emotional energy to that, which deafens her to other emotions about her marriage.
- If she will not take action to deal with the decay in her marriage, it will usually bleed over into anger toward others who cross her path. Often her children, whom God has given her to protect, become targets.

- When she does not know where her husband is, she feels not only panic but a loss of control as well. Fear and depression set in. If her husband is acting out and she is not taking godly action, she will repeat this cycle of panic, powerlessness, fear, and depression over and over again.

We are beings with God-given emotions. If we did not have some difficult emotions about the state of our marriages, we would be mere robots! However, we should not be completely ruled by our emotions. Allowing unbridled emotion to determine our behavior is self-destructive. Your husband may continue in his behavior, but you need to determine for yourself what the healthy response to it should be. Neither you nor your children should be the victims of his continued broken promises and betrayals. Consider the following scriptural insights:

A man without self-control is as defenseless as a city with broken-down walls. (Proverbs 25:28)

A wise woman builds her house, while a foolish woman tears hers down by her own efforts. (Proverbs 14:1)

* * * * * * * * * * * * * * * ✸ * * * * * * * * * * * * * *

Prayer for My Counterproductive Reactions

Lord, I've tried so many ways to fix my marriage on my terms. I need Your help and Your wisdom, to respond as You would. Help me overcome my fear and anxiety with courage and peace. I hand You the lead, so I can follow in Your steps to arrive at a better place than I ever could by my own doing. In Jesus Christ's name, amen.

* *

Further Resources
Love Is a Choice Workbook, Hemfeld, Minirth, et al. (Nashville: Thomas Nelson, 1991).

When a Boundary Is Breeched

*Putting confidence in an unreliable man is like chewing
with a sore tooth, or trying to run on a broken foot.*

<small>PROVERBS 25:19</small>

There are natural lines of respect which determine healthy boundaries in all relationships. In civilized society these boundaries are self-imposed demonstrations of decency toward one another. Women who have endured betrayal also *expected* certain things in marriage to be respected without necessarily verbalizing them. It wasn't until that respect was violated that they realized their partners have no self-imposed boundaries on certain hurtful behaviors.

When you discover your partner has crossed a natural boundary with his behavior, you should consider what other boundaries may be crossed in the future. This is why it's vitally important to determine where you can and cannot trust your husband.

To Trust or Not to Trust

Take this short true-or-false quiz:

- Trust is vital to encourage my husband in his recovery. (T/F)
- If I don't trust him, I haven't really forgiven him. (T/F)
- Trust is a command from God, something spouses must offer. (T/F)

The answer to all of the above statements is false. Why? Because genuine trust is an earned response to consistently kept promises and fulfilled expectations, it is either deserved or undeserved. It can't be manufactured or demanded, and it isn't commanded by God. It's determined by your personal experience with an individual based on his or her actions.

Some women have had the concept of trust turned inside out for so many years that the word has lost its meaning. A woman confused about trust may not trust her husband alone with her best friend but still trust her life and her children's lives to him as long as he provides for them.

Can you see a problem with this thinking?

One problem for many women is that trust gets commingled with forgiveness. The two are, in fact, completely separate issues. Forgiveness is offered as a gift. Your husband can't earn it. (We will study forgiveness in depth in volume 2.) But many a husband has pressured his wife to trust him by claiming this was a part of her forgiveness of his betrayals. The wife, obviously confused, may decide that this sounds pretty Christlike, so she goes along with it or at least tries to feign trust.

In an ideal recovery situation, even after a wife has forgiven her husband, she will still spend a few months or even a year or more determining if he can be trusted before she considers full reconciliation of the marriage. Marital trust involves huge risk as it is. After betrayal, all bets are off. Giving oneself ample time with firm boundaries is one of the wisest safeguards a woman can make, and it is a perfectly scriptural response to betrayal.

Trust Consistent Behavior

Trust must be earned by behavior. It requires being who you say you are and remaining consistent in that over time. If his words should mean little to you right now, that's to be expected. After all, though his *words* may have claimed he's a Christian, he's been *acting* like a pagan:

> It is God's will that you should…learn to control [your] own body in a way that
> is holy and honorable, not in passionate lust like the heathen, who do not know
> God. (1 Thessalonians 4:3–5, NIV).

When it comes to your husband's sexuality, his actions must eventually match up with his words. Until they do, he can't please God, and your trust in him will remain dead on arrival, no matter how hard you try to resurrect it on your own:

> The fact is that love, forgiveness, and commitment are choices that I can make alone in a vacuum, regardless of Fred's actions toward me. I can choose to love Fred simply by choosing to do so, no matter how he treats me. I can forgive Fred over and over even if he never asks me to. I can commit my heart faithfully to him no matter how adulterous his heart may grow in return.
>
> But trust can't exist in a vacuum like this. Trust can only exist in relationship. Oh, I can hope against hope that Fred'll keep his word…but real trust can only come when I have full confidence in Fred's faithfulness. Only one thing can bring that confidence—his consistent, faithful actions. My love, forgiveness, and commitment may require nothing of Fred, but my trust requires plenty. Without right actions, he can't have my trust, and if he wants my trust, it's all on him.
>
> Husbands often hate this responsibility, but you needn't apologize for it. And you needn't feel guilty if your husband sneers, "If you loved me, you would trust me." Baloney. Trust and love are two different things. (*Every Heart Restored*, 129–30)

From the Old Testament to the New, the human condition hasn't changed. Centuries ago, God was watching His people behave in ways that were contrary to their words.

> They remembered that God was their Rock—that their Savior was the God above all gods. But it was only with their words they followed him, not with their hearts; their hearts were far away. They did not keep their promises. Yet he was merciful and forgave their sins and didn't destroy them all. Many and many a time he held back his anger. For he remembered that they were merely mortal men, gone in a moment like a breath of wind. (Psalm 78:35–39)

Jesus also understood the frailty of the human condition. He knew that people, even those who love one another, were capable of betrayal when it served their own interest. Although He didn't trust people, He loved them and had fellowship with them. He just didn't expect more from them, as He knew the risk and the reality. "Jesus would not entrust himself to them, for he knew all men" (John 2:24, NIV). Extending trust in any relationship always involves some degree of risk of being hurt, rejected, or abandoned. There's no guarantee of not being wounded in a relationship, in marriage or in any other.

Having experienced betrayal of trust in your marriage, you know there are no fool-proof ways to guard against it. The best thing you can do is learn to walk with your eyes wide open. God wants to shine light in the dark places so you can see the truth. If you don't cover your eyes for fear of what you might see, you'll learn things about your husband's character through his actions. You'll learn if he's really changing from a betrayer into an honorable man of integrity.

You need to realize that the way back for your husband is a long and winding road, and just because you've determined to forgive and demonstrate God's love for him doesn't mean he should be trusted. Guarding your heart from any further wounding is, admittedly, an incredibly difficult thing to do when you're offering Christ's love to someone you don't trust.

Pray for wisdom in discerning when to trust again and when to set a boundary against potential injury. Remember, his consistent behavior must be your tangible measurement, not his words, not his one-time responses, not his attitudes. Believe only consistent behavior. Those with something to hide get by in life by becoming masters at convincing people (even themselves) that their lie is the truth. If you don't see the trustworthy behavior, don't make believe it is there.

> God's truth stands firm like a great rock, and nothing can shake it. It is a foundation stone with these words written on it: "The Lord knows those who are really his," and "A person who calls himself a Christian should not be doing things that are wrong." (2 Timothy 2:19)

We'll deal with more specific ways to know if he's trustworthy in the second volume of this study. For now, determine not to draw hasty conclusions based on faulty evidence, and look for the signs of true repentance.

MY · STONE · WORK

Insight

Go through the following list, carefully evaluating whether you can trust your husband with each area of your life according to his consistent behavior. Ask, *Can I trust him…*

- with my sexuality?
- with my pain?
- with my areas of weakness?
- with my/our children?
- with my spiritual life?
- during his alone time?
- with our money?
- when he's traveling alone?
- with co-workers?
- to keep his promises?
- with a hundred dollars?
- to nurture our children?

- to cherish me?
- with a credit card?
- with my love?
- with my friends/his friends?
- to tell me the truth?
- with his recovery?
- with my feelings?
- with our marriage vows?
- to do his job with integrity?
- with his responsibilities?
- to tell others the truth?
- to protect me?

After considering this list, do you find you're entrusting your husband in areas where he still hasn't proven trustworthy? In what place do you need to communicate a loving but firm boundary?

Action

Using this list, watch and record tangible behaviors that demonstrate your husband is becoming trustworthy in each area. If you don't see improvement over time in a particular area, be honest with him, but confront with love, and encourage him in areas where he's showing improvement.

When a husband has betrayed you, you're a victim of that betrayal. However, from that point on, you have a choice to make. You now have the information that he's not to be trusted until trust is rebuilt. If you decide to trust again without evidence of change, you're no longer a victim but a willing participant in your own injury. As Proverbs 14:15 says, "Only a simpleton believes what he is told! A prudent man checks to see where he is going." Trust building is a test of character with measurable results for the husband willing to prove himself trustworthy again. Waiting for the outcome will be a test in self-control for you.

Finally, as you saw in the list above, true trustworthiness extends far beyond physical fidelity. In reestablishing trust, we should make our decision to trust again in every area based on tangible measures. A person with an unchanged heart will still compromise in his behavior and integrity. It may be evident only in small matters, but don't dismiss the little things—they matter greatly. In trust, it's all or nothing: "Unless you are honest in small matters, you won't be in large ones. If you cheat even a little, you won't be honest with greater responsibilities" (Luke 16:10).

Other Important Boundaries

Of course, there are also the garden variety boundaries that most people struggle with. Have you ever felt guilty saying no to a request for help? Or have you said yes when you knew you shouldn't have and beat yourself up for it afterward? When the desire to please people becomes disruptive to you or your family, you have unhealthy boundaries.

However, here we'll focus on other destructive boundary violations beyond that grievous violation of sexual fidelity that may take place between a husband and wife living in varying degrees of dysfunction. For some, these kinds of breeches will seem shocking, while for others, many of these boundary violations are a regular part of their lives.

MY · STONE · WORK

Insight

Note those things that occur in your interaction with your husband.

Physical Boundary Breeches

- being touched in ways that make you uncomfortable
- being tickled without permission
- being restricted or held down against your will
- being manipulated to comply with what he wants you to wear
- being coerced to style or cut your hair a certain way
- being shamed into wearing more or less makeup than you would choose
- being scrutinized for every morsel of food you eat
- not being allowed to come and go at will
- being pushed, shoved, slapped, bitten, kicked, hit, punched, or choked
- being forced to stay awake

Emotional Boundary Breeches

- being told, "You shouldn't feel that way"
- having your feelings ignored
- being exposed to jealous anger that is unwarranted
- being threatened with abandonment or being forced to leave
- being called names
- having affection withheld as manipulation
- being exposed to uncontrolled rage
- being held responsible for his feelings ("You made me angry")
- being told you are responsible for his bad behavior
- not being allowed to cry
- being forced to stuff your feelings out of fear of violence

Intellectual Boundary Breeches

- being told you are crazy or stupid
- having your ability to reason things out for yourself discounted
- not being allowed to go back to school or work
- being told you will fail
- being blamed for your children's failures

- having your parenting abilities discounted
- not being allowed to make everyday choices
- having your speech or grammar constantly corrected
- having words put in your mouth

Spiritual Boundary Breeches

- having your relationship with God decided for you
- being belittled about your beliefs, your prayer life, your moral boundaries
- being manipulated and controlled by him through religion

Financial Boundary Breeches

- not being allowed to earn money
- being made responsible to handle financial obligations, while he spends without accountability
- having to cope with his use of household money to support his habit
- being forced to account for every cent you spend
- having his spending interfere with your and your children's welfare or health

If you were surprised to see many things that happen in your marriage on this list, you have been indoctrinated to believe that this is normal, justifiable behavior. A woman who is needy may easily become a victim, fearful of losing the relationship, and concede to abuse. For women who were abused as children, the dynamic often repeats in marriage. When a boundary violation occurs, she may feel helpless and defenseless again, unable to make appropriate decisions and act. Afterward she blames herself for the violation, just as she did as a child.

Action

The good news is that setting boundaries is a skill—it can be learned in tandem with healing of your own sense of worth in God's eyes. In the next chapter, we will continue to discuss this topic of boundaries to help you to put them into action.

Aren't Christian Wives
Supposed to Submit?

We'll deal specifically with submission in volume 2, but for now, consider this simple, yet profound, truth: God never calls us to overlook evil, endure abuse, or sacrifice our children for the sake of submitting to abusive treatment from a husband. In fact, His Word says, "Don't just pretend that you love others: really love them. Hate what is wrong. Stand on the side of the good" (Romans 12:9).

Passive submission only perpetuates evil. By not taking a stand and drawing proper boundaries, you are enabling your husband to continue his destructive behavior and remain in his delusion that this behavior is okay. There is nothing loving or godly about that.

Tolerating an abusive marriage is about trying to please a man rather than God. What motivates women to accept this sort of relationship? Primarily, a deep hunger for love and acceptance from a man. And it can be such a powerful force that woman literally discount the more important value of God's love and approval.

For they loved the praise of men more than the praise of God. (John 12:43)

. . . . ✺ . . . .

My Prayer
for Boundaries

I praise You, Lord, for Your perfect wisdom. Help me to be wise, to see evil for what it is. Show me how to protect my mind, my body, and my spirit from harmful people and circumstances. Reveal my motives for accepting unhealthy boundaries, Lord. Show me how to protect myself and loved ones from harm and how to guard my time with You. In Jesus's name, amen.

. . . .

Further Resources

Boundaries in Marriage, Henry Cloud and John Townsend (Grand Rapids: Zondervan, 1999).

Women Who Love Sex Addicts, Douglas Weiss and Dianne DeBusk (Fort Worth: Discovery, 1993).

Eighth Landmark

Boundary Enforcement

Have two goals: wisdom—that is, knowing and doing
right—and common sense. Don't let them slip away, for they
fill you with living energy, and are a feather in your cap. They
keep you safe from defeat and disaster and from stumbling
off the trail. With them on guard you can sleep without fear.

PROVERBS 3:21–24

When we do not take responsibility for our choices and refusal to set boundaries, we
make others responsible for them. I know I'm going to hear some loud disagreement,
but in some cases, your husband is not wholly responsible for your situation or your
emotions. Maybe you believe you're a victim of his whims, powerless to change the situation. But again, the Bible says, "It is for freedom that Christ has set us free. Stand firm,
then, and do not let yourselves be burdened again by a yoke of slavery" (Galatians 5:1,
NIV). We should not gratify the desires of the sinful nature: "sexual immorality, impurity and debauchery; idolatry and witchcraft; hatred, discord, jealousy, fits of rage, selfish ambition, dissensions, factions and envy; drunkenness, orgies, and the like" (verses
19–21). Doing so is what yokes us with a new enslavement. That slavery can be created
by idly enduring your husband's sinfulness (see list) or by placing a crown on your husband's head (idolatry), thereby putting his sinful desires above God's directives. Though
you may feel enslaved by your husband's behavior, you can make choices that can free
you from his destructiveness.

Our model for setting boundaries on others' behavior is God. The Bible shows that He sets limits on unrepentant people. We are to do the same, even when that person is our husband.

God expects us to seek out godly wisdom in tough situations. Healthy boundaries are scriptural and life giving. They help us to be mindful that we are human, that we have physical limitations and can't be everything to everyone. Unhealthy people either demand too much or give too much. We cause great harm to ourselves and others when we attempt to be too much or expect others to be too much.

Even Jesus placed limitations on His exposure to others. Look at some examples from the gospel of Mark (NIV):

- 1:35—"Very early…Jesus got up, left the house and went off to a solitary place, where he prayed." (He guarded His time with God.)
- 1:45—"Jesus could no longer enter a town openly but stayed outside in lonely places." (He protected Himself from overwhelming demands.)
- 3:7, 9—"Jesus withdrew with his disciples.… He told his disciples to have a small boat ready for him, to keep the people from crowding him." (He protected His body.)
- 3:13—"Jesus…called to him those he wanted." (He chose His companions.)
- 5:18–19—"The man…begged to go with him. Jesus did not let him." (He said no because He had other plans.)
- 6:31—"Because so many people were coming and going that they did not even have a chance to eat, he said to [his disciples], 'Come with me by yourselves to a quiet place and get some rest.'" (He took care of Himself emotionally and physically.)
- 9:30–31—"Jesus did not want anyone to know where they were, because he was teaching his disciples." (He guarded His need to do His work.)

Jesus's earthly ministry was the most important one of all time, yet He set boundaries to protect and guard His well-being. His is the model we should follow.

Boundaries Change Things

Imagine that a husband wants his wife to watch a pornographic video with him to spice things up in the bedroom. Knowing he's been more sexually aggressive recently, she is extremely uncomfortable about the idea but is naturally curious if this might give her a better idea of what's been influencing him. Look how two wives respond:

- Wife 1 agrees but feels guilty later. She consoles herself that at least she prevented him from going out and seeking satisfaction "God knows where."
- Wife 2 refuses and explains how she feels about his request. She asks him to accompany her to get counseling.

Wife 1 yokes herself with new sin and accompanying shame. Husband 1 continues his sin. Husband 2 can either agree or disagree with his wife, but regardless, she's upheld a boundary. However, if Husband 2 does reject Wife 2 and her request for counseling, she might, like Wife 1, conclude that setting boundaries doesn't work.

Yet the second scenario is the right choice because it's the only one in which the wife is safe from the effects of a potential breech to the marriage. Even if she is uncomfortable, she must follow the dictates of her conscience. And if her husband still decides to willingly sin, that decision will be his alone.

For most, retraining how you respond to breeches of your boundaries, after years of relating one way to your spouse, will take practice. But it starts by deciding how you want to be treated in a given situation.

MY · STONE · WORK

Insight

Get out the list of boundary violations in the previous chapter. For each boundary violation you've endured, give thought to, and write down, how you wish to be treated in the future. Write your wishes as affirmative statements (*I do want to be spoken of with respect*) rather than negative (*I don't want to be mocked in public*).

Congratulations! These statements are your new boundaries.

Your next step is to decide what consequence to apply when a boundary violation occurs. Write each consequence next to the corresponding boundary, and make this list one you can refer to regularly. An appropriate consequence for disrespect might read, *Leave for fifteen minutes, then seek an apology. No apology, no conversation for the rest of the day.*

Action

This is a challenge, but with practice, you can retrain yourself to stop accepting destructive behaviors from others and bring health to yourself, your children, and your marriage. If this feels extremely foreign to you, work with your walking companion or counselor, first to affirm that your boundaries are reasonable lines of respect, and secondly, to role-play situations that arise with your husband.

Consequences Aren't Optional

Boundaries and consequences for violations go hand in hand. Without consequences, a violator has no motivation to change his behavior. Imagine if police didn't enforce the laws. The laws would become meaningless.

When God hears you say, *I can't live this way anymore,* His response is, *Great! Don't! I never wanted you to live like that.* One of the strongest consequences that you may need to consider is a separation from your husband. Later in this guidebook, you will traverse all the pathways of considering a godly separation. Whatever boundaries and consequences you need to enforce, doing so will take time and strength, but stay the course. Going God's way vastly improves your possibility of renewing the marriage. Remember, boundaries are loving—even when tough. Passivity is selfish and forces you to forfeit both love and freedom.

Drs. Henry Cloud and John Townsend say in their book, *Boundaries* (Grand Rapids: Zondervan, 2002, pages 135–36), that boundaries are in no way intended to put an end to love. They are meant to do just the opposite: gain back your freedom to genuinely love. When you are bound by fear of another person's reaction to the appropriate boundaries you might set, you are not truly free to love.

It is good to sacrifice and deny yourself for the sake of others, but in order to freely make that choice you need to set good boundaries. Yet this can be overdone also. Sometimes people who are just beginning to build boundaries feel that to do anyone a favor is codependent. Nothing is further from the truth! Doing a good deed for another, when you freely choose to do it, is boundary enhancing. Codependents are not doing good freely. They are allowing evil because they are afraid.

The Other Side of the Wall

Finally, as you learn to take back your free will and enforce personal boundaries, make sure you exercise personal discipline and decide not to be a violator of others' boundaries as well.

MY · STONE · WORK

Insight

Some of the behaviors I listed in chapters 5 and 6 concerned a woman's lack of personal boundaries. Go back and review the lists, focusing on areas where your own lack of self-imposed boundaries could use some support. Be aware when you're with friends, family, or co-workers of ways you may lack self-control. Do you manipulate, get angry, shame others, pout, or give others the silent treatment to get your way? Or maybe you simply seethe inwardly. Write down any behaviors you think may need adjusting, and ask your walking companion or a close friend if there are ways you routinely invade their boundaries. Write down any insights you receive. "It is a badge of honor to accept valid criticism" (Proverbs 25:12).

Action

Commit yourself to practicing healthy boundaries every day to make lasting changes in your relationships with friends and family. As you learn to

---

control yourself in the same way you're asking your husband to control himself, the boundary issues you face with your husband will become less difficult.

My Prayer to Enforce Boundaries

Lord, help me to see boundaries from Your perspective. Some enforcing seems harsh and unloving. Help me to be a godly woman, instead of worrying so much about hurting the feelings of an unfeeling offender. Help me to end my passivity and stand up for godliness. Help me to love Your way. In Jesus's name, amen.

Further Resources

Angry Men and the Women Who Love Them, Paul Hegstrom (Kansas City, MO: Beacon Hill, 2004).

Ninth Landmark

Why a Man Takes This Detour

Before every man there lies a wide and pleasant road he
thinks is right, but it ends in death.

PROVERBS 16:25

Sexual betrayal can come in many forms. One man furtively views "soft porn" on the Internet; another husband may be obsessed with harder pornography. Betrayal may take the form of a brief affair, a long-standing relationship, or serial affairs throughout the marriage. Some men pursue many forms of sexual betrayal, others only one. Yet they all detour down that wide road for one reason: to fill a void.

The void may have a different source for each man. But the bottom line is that each experienced a lack of love in relationships, from others, God, or both. In some instances, a loving relationship may have been offered, but he wasn't willing or able to find satisfaction from it. For other cases, a disconnect comes because his wife doesn't understand his needs. I am not implying that a wife is to then hold blame for her husband's sin. Read on.

We're All Different

In general, the way men view and experience sex is fundamentally different from the way women do. In the simplest terms, sex is the way men experience love or intimacy. For women, in contrast, sex is a response to love and intimacy. That's not to suggest that men don't have loving feelings apart from the sexual experience. But sex for a man creates feelings of love and intimacy. In his book *Love and Respect,* Dr. Emerson Eggerichs says,

> The point here is that your husband's anatomy and design is much different from yours. He needs sexual release as you need emotional release. This is why he loves the act of sex in and of itself. It is a pleasurable act that brings him satisfaction. As a woman, you may feel that the two of you have to feel and be close in order to share sexually. For him, however, it is the reverse: the sexual act is what brings the two of you close!" (page 253)

In other words, sex enhances a man's love for his wife. Again generally speaking, a man may see one of the biggest benefits of getting married as the available sexual connection and companionship with the woman he loves. For women, getting married is about a continual source of romance and financial security. God built those drives in the two genders differently. Neither is wrong; they are just different.

Most women are surprised to learn that the average man thinks about sex many times a day. That's because the average man has a more urgent sex drive than women have. He is also much more apt to be visually stimulated to sexual arousal than a woman. Unlike most women, many men identify their masculinity with their feelings of success in the bedroom. Though men are physically bigger and stronger than women, their emotions are more fragile and vulnerable when it comes to sharing how they feel.

A man may succumb to sexual temptation for a variety of reasons, and the previous paragraph alludes to most of them. A purely physical attraction to another person is one possible reason. That temptation might be hardest to resist if the door has been left open by unfulfilled sexual desire. Feelings of insecurity are another possible reason. A man whose ego is feeling insecure may succumb because another shows interest in him and makes him feel special.

Acceleration

The man who enters into an affair or dabbles in pornography, if caught or convicted of his sin early on, may not have become entrenched in a dangerous and flawed belief system. Some men will end their journeys down the path of betrayal, though they caused heartache. If the wife has any willingness to restore the marriage, both partners will have to work on learning how to meet each other's needs in healthy ways. A great starting point would be to read *Love and Respect* together or to experience a seminar with Dr. Eggerichs and his wife, Sarah (check LoveandRespect.com for availability).

Other men continue to stagger down that path of sexual sin, headed for destruction. When husband and wife don't understand how to meet each other's needs, or the husband feels unsafe expressing emotion, he may become wary of the vulnerability of the relationship. This fear of rejection keeps him traveling down a hazard-filled road with the flawed equation that *any* sex is love. Sex will eventually become his greatest perceived need.

Sex that's void of healthy relationship can easily become a man's coping mechanism. There are varying degrees of preoccupation, from lusting for someone walking by to acting out sexually several times a day. And whether you call it habit, compulsiveness, or addiction, all these terms describe the same problem—repeatedly using sexual release the same way that alcoholics use alcohol.

Understand that no one gets ensnared in this destructive behavior overnight. As sex becomes a dependable means of avoidance, it causes a man to reject the only true way of enduring life's pain—dependence on God. And when someone rejects a relationship with God, God respects that person's free will and gives him or her over—spirit, body, and soul—to what the person has chosen.

A biblical view of sexual obsession can be found in Romans 1. This chapter of Scripture shows what causes such driven desire. It's summed up in the phrases, "God also gave them up" and "God gave them over" to their desires (verses 24 and 28, NKJV). God removed His hand of protection from them and allowed their idols to reign over them. The only real power the idols had was that which humans gave them. The human body and sex itself have become this kind of idol.

In this way, the very thing the man thought would free him takes him captive. By attempting to take control, he loses exactly what he was trying to gain. No one likes being called an addict, but Dr. Harry Schaumberg (*False Intimacy*, 57), who has studied sexual compulsivity for years, uses the term *addict* without apology. He says we must realize that sex addiction is an extension of our common fallen natures. Thinking of addiction as a disease may ease the burden of guilt on the deviant but it isn't accurate. It negates choice. At some point prior to addiction, deviants choose to use sexual fulfillment to compensate for emotional pain. And eventually, they come to equate sex with love and that they can't live without it. Sex addicts create the illusion that what their souls crave can be completely satisfied through sex. They become highly motivated because sex is how they find relief. Thus, to stop their behavior seems like a death sentence.

However, the feeling of having control over the pain is elusive, which causes addicts to repeatedly deepen their addiction. And as with any drug, as an addict's tolerance to it develops, desperation begins to set in, which leads the addict to further actions to fulfill his or her need.

But My Husband Says...

Most women believe on some level that a husband's compulsive behavior has to do with a defect in the wife. Once again, this logic is faulty. If your husband has deluded himself into believing the lies, he may lay the blame at your feet. But the truth is that he has rejected your love, intimacy, openness, and vulnerability, just as he has rejected God. Though you both may have been unaware of how to best meet each other's needs, he chose to detour away from what seemed to be landmines loaded with difficult emotions instead of risking honesty to talk about his frustrations and find solutions together.

Despite what he really desires, he's found it easier, less frightening, or more reliable to pursue false intimacy. Imaginary partners are much more reliable than real ones. Maybe the substitute is more understanding of his needs, always available, and asks nothing of him in return. And as time marches on in this make-believe world, he cements his fear of honest, open relationship.

This is why believing sex with you isn't "enough for him" is a bit like believing water isn't enough to quench an alcoholic's thirst. Of course water isn't enough—his soul needs stronger medicine to numb the pain. His thirst is something that pure water can't quench. He needs his fix, so he has to keep going back to the polluted well.

Loving, intimate, relational sex between husband and wife is the only kind that truly quenches, but many live with a deep shame that, to them, seems to call for a stronger medicine. So they accept a system that brings "intimacy" without risk and offers total control over their "partners." But soon, they find they have anything but control over themselves.

You see, the genuine need a guy has for interpersonal intimacy cannot be met by self-seeking sexual activity. His original itch for genuine intimacy can't be scratched or satisfied by porn and masturbation—it only feels that way for a fleeting moment. In the end, his heart is left itching, and all he does is head back to the computer for some substitute intimacy, which drives him further within himself, which leaves him itching and feeling emptier…and so the downward spiral goes. In his book for men caught in this spiral, Fred Stoeker wrote,

> If you get caught up in Internet porn…you'll be like a dog chasing his tail. The cycle will be endless. Once you turn inward and fixate on porn and masturbation—and yourself—your problems only compound as your sense of disconnection deepens. (*Tactics*, 95–96)

The apostle Paul put it another way: "I don't understand myself at all, for I really want to do what is right, but I can't. I do what I don't want to—what I hate" (Romans 7:15).

Wounds of Childhood

Many wounds originate in childhood and were caused by the very people God intended to love and protect us: our parents. For most men, the broadest, most jagged wounds come from their fathers:

> This was no ordinary wound. There was a gaping hole of inadequacy [from my dad] that left me feeling lonely and cut off from the rest of the world. That's one reason why I went looking for love—and my manhood—elsewhere. I found it in bed with young women. Remember what I said about the primary way that guys give and receive intimacy? It's in the things we do with a woman prior to

and during sexual intercourse.... My dad wasn't there for me...so I was left to sort out my manhood by paging through porn magazines and touching willing women. Needless to say, that approach worked out miserably for me. (*Tactics,* 104–5)

The people God intended to be our first examples of unconditional love, healthy dependence, and discipline sometimes harm us and skew our understanding of God. When a child lives with a harsh or neglectful parent, he comes to believe God can't be trusted, that His love is conditional. He tends to adopt a similar view of other close relationships.

Some...children become emotionally numb, unwilling to risk, seeking to control the amount of pleasure and pain in their lives. Children who learn to bury their emotions deep inside—who deny their true feelings—are candidates for sexual addiction because false intimacy brings sensations, activity, and excitement that counter their paralyzed inner feelings. If a child grows up believing that true intimacy isn't possible, that fulfillment in life isn't attainable, and that emotions are to be feared, that child may choose false intimacy. (*False Intimacy,* 65)

No average female or simple bedroom sex can begin to compare to the images before him and to where his imagination has taken him. An adolescent boy, shy around real girls, feels awkward in his attempts to have meaningful female friendships and fears girls' rejection. He finds a pretense of comfort, love, and excitement in a fictional world of perfect female images. He can create a fantasy relationship where there is no risk of rejection. She has no personal needs, but she knows exactly what he needs emotionally and physically and fulfills those needs in his imaginary world. A young man will masturbate and bond to these images in his head; in doing so, he taps into a euphoric physical chemistry that was meant to be reserved as a gift to be shared in the union of marriage....

Single men who have given themselves permission to satisfy their urges and are already in the habit of using substitutes are often of the false belief that they will no longer be interested in these activities once they are married. They believe that having the availability of a sexual partner 24/7 will give them the outlet they desire for sexual activity. What they don't take into account is that they have conditioned their minds for a specific type of stimuli; these extramarital sexual activities don't require anything of them in the forging and nurturing of a relationship. *Lovemaking* with a marriage partner is about *giving* to your spouse. The sexual activities the sexual addict has become accustomed to are all about *taking* for self-gratification.

It's Just Pornography

The definition of *pornography* is "the depiction of erotic behavior intended to cause sexual excitement." *Erotic* means "arousing sexual desires." In other words, any image created for sexual arousal is pornography. Many of us have been so desensitized that we've forgotten how prevalent porn actually is.

When sexual arousal comes from someplace or someone other than one's spouse, it invites comparison. And unfortunately, the spouse loses in this game because no one can compete with perfect images devoid of imperfect personality or difficult emotion. This leads to further dissatisfaction with the spouse. Consider the three most common myths about pornography:

MYTH: Sexual fantasy doesn't affect real relationships.

FACT: Fantasies come from desires. What we desire influences our thinking. Such fantasies also commonly involve the lure of sex without attachment, which is opposed to relationship and causes destructive behavior.

MYTH: Porn can be a good education in sex and increase enjoyment.

FACT: Sure, pornography teaches, but it teaches much that is false and misleading as well. Its twisted view of human sexuality fails to depict true female sexual nature and response, as well as presenting scenarios in which intimacy is irrelevant to sexuality.

MYTH: Pornography increases one's ability to satisfy a lover.

FACT: Whether it's produced for men or for women, the underlying focus of pornography validates selfish desires, which actually *decreases* the ability to satisfy a lover. It shortens foreplay, replaces it with impatience to get to the finish line, and increases premature ejaculation, incidence of rape, and even marital violence. (This information is adapted from Victor B. Cline, "Pornography's Effect on Adults and Children," New York: Morality in Media, 2001.)

Internet Porn—the Crack Cocaine of Sex

In our culture, men used to risk social embarrassment if they purchased pornographic materials. Yet with the Internet, times have changed. Today, even men who don't share the common risk factors for sex addiction can easily become addicted. To the natural allure of visual stimulation that men share, the Internet adds three more elements: access, anonymity, and affordability. And this combination opens the door to a fourth element: acceleration.

The Internet is the primary reason sex addiction is quickly becoming a worldwide social epidemic. It is also the reason we are seeing such a widespread desensitization to pornography. Simple curiosity when rewarded with pleasure can even more quickly turn to fascination and eventually obsession.

Consider how easily the cycle of sex obsession can trap a person. Curiosity leads to fascination, which can easily become preoccupation. The individual develops a habit he feels ashamed about, and he exercises some control so he won't go "too far." Yet over time his control wanes, and his preoccupation demands action. When he finally gives in, he feels more shame, and the resulting emotional pain demands stronger medication.

Eventually, he begins to sense he is "defective" or deviant, and he berates himself into another phase of temporary self-discipline, regaining a sense of control over his behavior.

Some go through the full cycle every few months, others more frequently. During the self-control phase of the cycle, a man may convince himself—and those around him—that he no longer has the problem. But it's only temporary. He is considering changing his ways and getting help because he realizes the medication isn't working as it used to, but he still doesn't know how to replace it with true intimacy.

Common Behaviors

The most common behavior of the sexually obsessed is masturbation. Orgasm brings a quick jolt of euphoric release, a temporary escape from bottled up emotional pain.

I've found most women are unaware of what a large role masturbation plays in boy's or men's lives. It's so easy for him to hide it—even in his own home. The truth, however, isn't lost on the porn empire, which has become one of the most lucrative industries in the world selling masturbation tools disguised as "male entertainment."

Why is the lure so powerful? Just like all sinful behaviors, it does provide a certain level of pleasure or meet some internal need, although the effect is fleeting. This behavior would not be tempting if it did not produce some instant gratification. Following is a list of behaviors commonly used by the sex-obsessed individual:

- visual stimulation, usually resulting in masturbation during or shortly after exposure: the person walking down the street; pictures in a man's mind that he pulls up on demand; magazines, catalogs, videos, television, movies, Web sites, and live shows
- verbal stimulation, usually resulting in masturbation during or shortly after exposure: phone sex, calls to escort services and "massage" ads, Web chat rooms
- physical contact: prostitutes, one-time encounters, an ongoing affair

Says Schaumberg, "Sadly, such behavior invariably creates far more intense pain than the original pain the addict is trying to escape and/or prevent" (*False Intimacy,* 49).

The Good News

The disease model of the addict that the professional psychiatric community embraces concludes, "once an addict, always an addict." What this conclusion leaves out is the healing and restoration that comes from one Source offering us complete redemption. When we come to Christ for healing, we no longer have to be defined by our past sins.

The biblical model of restoration reveals that sex, alcohol, or food is not the addict's real problem. The real problem lies in the heart. The abused substance is merely a tool to gain control over pain rather than turning to God for help and comfort.

The great news is that a sexually obsessed individual can be healed and then be able to resume an intimate, monogamous sexual relationship. He is not a "sex addict who is clean and sober"; he is a new creation in Christ. He doesn't "fall off the wagon" when he has sex with his wife. When a man's heart is changed, sex is no longer a dark cave he enters to escape from pain. It is a safe dwelling where he can nurture intimacy.

What's Normal?

Sexual behavior is and always will be cloaked in mystery. Add to that natural mystery the misinformation communicated by our culture's media and your husband's skewed perspective, and it's easy to feel like your sex life falls short. The following list is not intended to ensure you're meeting the national averages but to help you define what is biblically sound. The most important aspect of any sex life is that it be nurturing to both partners' emotional, physical, and spiritual intimacy. This is not a comprehensive examination, but only the most commonly discussed aspects from our national Avenue groups.

Intercourse

God tells us to have sex regularly to prevent temptation to fulfill our needs elsewhere. Twice a week is considered healthy for a marriage, based on an average of men's and women's natural desire levels and physical abilities. Of course, many men could have sex every day. Yet many women neither desire nor can physically handle such frequency. Everyone goes through natural stages and periods when sex is either more or less frequent. For both partners, it's important to take the long view of the seasons of a relationship rather than to needlessly worry about a temporary change in sexual energy, stamina, or desire.

From God's point of view, the most important thing to remember is this:

> The husband should give to his wife her conjugal rights (goodwill, kindness, and what is due her as his wife), and likewise the wife to her husband. For the wife does not have [exclusive] authority and control over her own body, but the husband [has his rights]; likewise also the husband does not have [exclusive] authority and control over his body, but the wife [has her rights]. Do not refuse and

deprive and defraud each other [of your due marital rights], except perhaps by mutual consent for a time, so that you may devote yourselves unhindered to prayer. But afterwards resume marital relations, lest Satan tempt you [to sin] through your lack of restraint of sexual desire. (1 Corinthians 7:3–5, AMP)

Women need to pay attention in order to nurture a satisfying sex life with their husbands. Generally speaking, it is the woman who puts low priority on sex, especially when children come along or a demanding career competes for her time and energy. Remember, for a Christian *normal* means to be like Christ. While Christ was never married, we know that Jesus was the Word in flesh, so we also know that when we follow the Word of God, we will always be like Christ. We need to follow this passage if we are to have a normal sexual relationship before God:

What was God's intent [in this passage]? That neither party would have total control of their yes or their no in the marriage bed. For instance, sex under the total control of the husband's yes isn't God's plan. If the husband is consistently forcing his wife to have sex against her will, then something is wrong with the relationship.

At the same time, the wife can't have full control of her no, always waiting until she's in the mood. If the husband is being consistently forced to *not* have sex against his will, then something is just as wrong with the relationship. Neither is normal, and God wanted us to know that. (*Every Heart Restored,* 223–24)

Foreplay

Women's bodies need the emotional "switch" of foreplay before intercourse. The natural, physical response of arousal can come from physical, verbal, or even emotional or mental stimuli as when a woman experiences deep attraction through thoughts or feelings. Some studies indicate that men, too, require foreplay to experience the true goal of emotional intimacy that orgasm alone can't supply.

Variety

Style of sex, location, time of day, and duration should vary. No one enjoys the same meal every day—and fast-food "quickies" are a part of variety. Yet they should be part of a healthy diet that includes well-rounded meals. The guiding principle when it comes to sexual variety is to ensure it is both healthful and enjoyable for both involved.

Oral Sex

There is no biblical prohibition against oral sex, and it is spoken of in veiled poetic terms in the Song of Solomon. It can be a part of foreplay or an occasional substitute for intercourse, adding another enjoyable dimension of variety. However, individuals who don't enjoy it should never be pressured or coerced. If you or your husband has a problem with oral sex, there is likely an underlying reason, and the loving response is to work toward mutual understanding.

Playfulness

At its best, sex is about "making love." This can only happen when two people are completely comfortable and relaxed with each other. Laughter, gentle wrestling, and shared humor should play a part in healthy sex. From intimacy grows joy, and couples who are closely connected and comfortable with themselves and each other develop a unique and private form of communication that has specific meaning to them. This continues to develop over the years and doesn't happen without intentional and sincere effort of sharing one's true, uninhibited self.

Sensual Clothing

This can add mystery, enticement, and variety to a committed couple's lovemaking. Yet again, no one should be coerced into anything that causes discomfort. Here, as in other areas, the goal is to offer oneself freely. Specific clothing should never be required or relied on to produce excitement.

What's Not Normal?

Threesomes

Either real or imagined, third parties ruin intimacy. Pornography, adult videos, sexual aids, and even masturbation invite a third-party intrusion. All these activities involve a person or thing other than your spouse fulfilling your sexual needs. Threesomes never lead to deeper shared intimacy.

Obscene Language
This has no place in lovemaking. While sex sometimes elicits frank language, using vulgar or coarse words is degrading to the loveliness of sexuality.

Fetishes
Any object that is *required* in order for husband or wife to be stimulated, such as high heels or other specific garments or objects, is a form of idolatry and interferes like a third-party intrusion on committed, monogamous sex.

Sodomy
Sodomy is only referred to in the Bible as an act between two men or with prostitutes. And wherever it is mentioned, God prohibits it. Further, health issues, hygiene, and the potential for internal damage seem to make anal intercourse unnatural in marital relations as well.

Domination
Sex forced on a person is considered rape, even in marriage. Any coerced or manipulative sex that involves exerting control over one's partner is just as sinful. Domination is the opposite of a loving, sacrificial expression and has no place in lovemaking.

Masturbation
Masturbation is not addressed in the Bible, so we need to look to principles. Solo sex breeds isolation, not intimacy; that's the opposite of God's plan. Some women ask us, "Is it okay for my husband to masturbate as long as he's only thinking about me when he does it?" Consider this e-mail from Kayla:

> I asked my husband recently if masturbation continues to be a problem for him.
> After dancing around the question for a couple of minutes, he agreed that it still
> is a problem, on occasion (whatever that means!). He seems to be all right with

this, but I am not. He insists it's always me he thinks about while masturbating, so that makes it okay. I have my doubts that he only thinks of me, but even if he is only thinking about me, haven't I just been reduced to a pornographic image in his mind, and doesn't that sex act still only serve him and his desires?

Kayla hit the nail on the head. When a husband pleads for permission from you to masturbate as long as he's thinking of you, he's simply trying to maintain one last corner of control over his sexuality. When it comes to the effects of this kind of masturbation on his sexuality and upon your intimacy as a couple, there is no difference between this kind and any other kind of masturbation. It is still all about medication, and it is still all about him.

An Unwelcome Inheritance

Many men in the recovery process realize that their own fathers had or have the same sexual and intimacy issues. Prior to recognizing the compulsive nature of such behavior, they were probably not aware of the full extent of their fathers' behaviors. They may have been angry that their fathers were cheating on their mothers without recognizing the compulsive nature of the behavior nor the impact it was unconsciously having on them, as it often repeats in families.

Throughout history, the sexual betrayer has gone by many names as attitudes changed: cad, philanderer, ladies' man, skirt chaser, playboy, womanizer, player, pimp, sex machine, skunk. These terms used for men with the same behavior acknowledge sin's repetitive nature. It shouldn't surprise us that sons will follow in their fathers' footsteps. As the Bible says, "I will bring the curse of a father's sins upon even the third and fourth generation of the children of those who hate me" (Deuteronomy 5:9–10).

But look at the last line of this passage: "But I will show kindness to a thousand generations of those who love me." Anyone willing to break the chain of idol worship and seek God's heart has this hope, regardless of family history. Any pattern of infidelity in a family can be rejected by choosing God's ways. We can use the authority God gives us to renounce this curse. Even if you aren't sure whether your husband's sin is generational, use this prayer to help work through this "housekeeping."

My Prayer to Cast Away Generational Sin

Dear heavenly Father, I reject and disown all the sins of my ances-
tors. In the power of the blood of Jesus Christ, I command every
familiar spirit and enemy to flee my presence and my home, never
to return. I close the door on all attempts of the Enemy to continue
this sinful legacy. I declare myself eternally and completely a child
of Your holy family. I ask You to fill me now with Your Holy
Spirit, that You may dwell in me and my house forever. Thank
You, Lord, for giving me the protection of Your presence, that I
may call on You to rescue me and bring me to Your holy ground. In
Jesus Christ's name, amen.

If he is willing, your husband can use this prayer as well. If he is involved with
Avenue for Men, he will deal with this issue in his study.

Social Ramifications

What sets marriage apart from all other relationships is the sexual union. It is the seal
on the covenant, like the circle of wax keeping an important envelope closed, private,
and exclusive.

Imagine the old wax seals that ensured only the intended recipient saw what was
inside. It ensured the content's authenticity and underscored its importance. If the
seal was broken, the security was destroyed. The message inside could no longer be
trusted.

Why do all civilized societies have laws dealing with adultery? The intact family
unit is the foundation of civilization, the container of uniquely precious contents. History has taught us, again and again, that as the value of family is destroyed in a society,
so that society is as well.

A woman wrestling with her husband's betrayals may focus on the physical act of her husband's betrayal. Another woman might be most distraught because of the emotional intimacy that he shared with another. Yet another wife may be most angered at his actions in light of the fact that "he calls himself a Christian."

Every person is comprised of three natures: body, soul, and spirit. I will discuss that in depth in the landmark "Getting Your Needs Met." For now, though, keep those in mind as we look at scriptures describing how sexual compromise affects each nature; not one is left untouched. "Whoever commits adultery with a woman lacks understanding; he who does so destroys his own soul" (Proverbs 6:32, NKJV). The soul is that part of us that makes up our characters, our emotions, our minds.

The last line in the next scripture explains why sexual compromise is so destructive to the soul. "From within, out of men's hearts, come evil thoughts of lust, theft, murder, adultery, wanting what belongs to others, wickedness, deceit, lewdness, envy, slander, pride, and all other folly. All these vile things come from within; they are what pollute you and make you unfit for God" (Mark 7:21–23). If we consider ourselves Christians, what could be more devastating to our minds and hearts than being "unfit for God"? These harmful thoughts, in and of themselves, are sin. And for some, these thoughts are acted out in the flesh, resulting in further destruction:

> Do you not know that your bodies are members of Christ himself? Shall I then take the members of Christ and unite them with a prostitute? Never! Do you not know that he who unites himself with a prostitute is one with her in body? For it is said, "The two will become one flesh." But he who unites himself with the Lord is one with him in spirit.
>
> Flee from sexual immorality. All other sins a man commits are outside his body, but he who sins sexually sins against his own body. Do you not know that *your body is a temple of the Holy Spirit,* who is in you, whom you have received from God? You are not your own; you were bought at a price. Therefore honor God with your body. (1 Corinthians 6:15–20, NIV)

When a person indulges in sexual sin, that person raids another's temple, wanting *what belongs to another.* At the same time, the person pollutes and raids her own temple, stealing from God and from herself. Pieces of ourselves—body, soul, and spirit—are given away and taken from others. Ironically, the phrase "get a piece?" is more literal than figurative. Realize that though we plunder from others' temples, we don't add anything of value to ours; we reap only destruction.

What does temple raiding cost us? When our temples are occupied with our sinful pollution, we crowd out the Holy Spirit: "For God did not call us to be impure, but to live a holy life. Therefore, he who rejects this instruction does not reject man but God, who gives you his Holy Spirit" (1 Thessalonians 4:7–8, NIV). When we reject Him, hearing from the Holy Spirit becomes extremely difficult. We don't receive His wisdom, and there is neither room nor nourishment for growth of the fruits of the Spirit. "When the Holy Spirit controls our lives he will produce this kind of fruit in us: love, joy, peace, patience, kindness, goodness, faithfulness, gentleness and self-control" (Galatians 5:22–23). When we live in a raided temple, we lose out on real love, real joy, and all these attributes that are the essence of an abundant life. Do you see how the person who compromises himself sexually is affected—body, soul, and spirit?

MY · STONE · WORK

Insight

While your husband probably has more repair work to do than you first thought, you yourself may have a history of extramarital promiscuity. If that applies to you, and if you have not before, take this time to bring to mind any sexual sin. If your list is long, write these things on a separate piece of paper instead of in your journal.

Action

Use this as a chance to seek God's forgiveness for sexual sin in your life. Here is a prayer to help you:

My Prayer to Restore the Raided Temple

Dear heavenly Father, You have told us to make no provision for the flesh in regard to its lusts. I confess that I have given in to sexual sin in my longing for love or acceptance or pleasure. I confess that I [name your specific sins]. I ask Your forgiveness for my actions. I have transgressed Your will for my life. I humbly thank You for Your undeserved forgiveness and mercy. I ask You to cleanse this place of all impurity and show me how to rebuild my temple by Your design. I surrender to Your plan to make my body a temple in which the Holy Spirit would love to dwell. Father, please sever all the unholy uniting and restore that which was lost to my raids. As Your daughter, I know I can't succeed on my own; heal me—body, soul, and spirit. In Your strength, I will flourish as I fill this new temple with the fruits of the Spirit. Through the cleansing of the blood of the Lord Jesus Christ, amen.

As soon as you are done praying, take your paper and burn it in a fire-safe area (such as a fireplace). In the future, if any old sin comes to your thoughts, remind yourself that you have been forgiven. Don't dwell on the offense or on any person with whom you had an unholy union.

Shame on Me, Shame on You

Those who look to him are radiant; their faces are never covered with shame. (Psalm 34:5, NIV)

Does that passage strike you as odd? What's shame got to do with it?

Consider this: your husband may carry childhood shame from misdirected anger, abuse, or neglect. He carries old sin as well. It may not be a conscious thing, but that legacy of sin can make him feel less worthy than others, and that is shame.

The natural response to shame is to hide its source behind secrets, phoniness, and a rejection of intimacy. Unless adolescent shame is consciously dealt with, a man carries it into adulthood.

You may have brought your own cloak of shame into your marriage. It isn't uncommon for such women to unconsciously choose a mate who can't or won't be intimate either. Wanting a partner, but not wanting to risk too much, maybe you've kept secrets and even lied about certain areas of your life to avoid the pain and risk of being hurt again.

Or you may be experiencing shame from behaviors your husband has drawn you into. But even if you don't have those kinds of shame, a woman who's been betrayed is still likely to carry some shame. And her husband may help her along—blaming her for his behavior. If you accept that shame, it will work to keep you in isolation. It will keep you from dealing with the real issues in your marriage and getting the help you need and from developing deep relationships with friends and God. Don't let shame trap you.

MY · STONE · WORK

Insight

Take time now to journal about any experiences you may have had that brought you shame. Starting with your early life history, what things have caused you to feel shame? Write specifically about anything you said or did or things said or done to you. What kinds of things have you done in response to that shame? Have you hidden from relationships or pulled back when things became too intimate?

Action

God wants us to expose the places where we hide from shame. During the course of this study, discuss the sources of your shame with your walking companion or in your study group. Allow others to help you remove that cloak of shame that's been hiding your true beauty. Remember, you have the authority through Jesus to rebuke any cruel words that have stuck to you and renounce unhealthy beliefs you've adopted. Ask God to show you His thoughts and desires for you. It is not Him but the Adversary who convinces you to hide from others in shame.

One More Thing

This is a difficult chapter for many women: *More information than I really wanted, thank you.* You may feel tempted to run. Other women find that understanding their husbands' struggles helps them see their situations with more compassion. If you're experiencing new emotions as a result of reading this chapter, be sure to journal about them, and consider any appropriate responses you might make.

Practically speaking, if you have any reason to believe your husband has had sexual involvement with another, determine to get tested for sexually transmitted diseases and request that your husband do the same. Don't allow fear to rule over you. There are twenty-five STDs! If you are unwilling to go to your family doctor because of embarrassment, go somewhere out of town. Health-care practitioners are schooled in privacy issues. Testing is a daily request; it won't raise eyebrows. Doctors will explain what testing is available and recommended. If this is your situation, I suggest that you absolutely refuse sex with your husband until both of you receive clear test results.

For most women in your situation, abstinence is a foregone conclusion. Where there's no trust, abstinence can be the healthiest, most reasonable position. It is not about retaliation or punishment. Nor is it necessarily about withdrawing from the relationship. When a husband has engaged in sex beyond marriage, abstinence is simply the reasonable consequence for his behavior, the result of his own decisions, and is a wise health choice. In this case, a commitment to abstinence on your part right now is the best way to allow for the possibility of a new foundation for healthy intimacy.

. . . . ✺ . . . .

My Prayer for Healthy Sexuality

Dear heavenly Father, thank You for showing me how walking through life without You leads to a dead end. Grow my compassion for my husband, in spite of the hurt he has caused me. Restore what's been broken, and heal all the wounds that caused him to seek out false intimacy. Show me the way back to Your view of sexuality, the beautiful and sacred union You intended. Remove my cloak of shame, and bring me the help, guidance, and support I need to find a better place. Show me how to be intimate again and allow affection, in its proper place and time. In Jesus Christ's name, amen.

. . . .

Further Resources

False Intimacy, Harry Schaumberg, PhD (Colorado Springs: NavPress, 1994).

The Bondage Breaker, Neil T. Anderson (Eugene, OR: Harvest House, 1990).

Intimate Issues, Linda Dillow and Lorraine Pintus (Colorado Springs: WaterBrook, 1999).

Love and Respect, Emerson Eggerichs (Brentwood, TN: Integrity, 2004).

The Whole Truth...in Love

A prudent man foresees the difficulties ahead and prepares
for them; the simpleton goes blindly on and suffers the
consequences.

PROVERBS 22:3

When the first crack in the facade appears, some truth leaks out. It may be something
you discover. It may be something a third party tells you. Or it may come as a confession from your husband himself.

No matter how it's delivered, the truth comes with some degree of pain and often
anger and humiliation. Sometimes it comes as a complete shock. Other times, it validates your suspicions.

Generally speaking, a truly addicted husband's first confession is just the tip of the
iceberg, and there's much more underneath. But before you demand the whole truth,
you need to consider whether you're ready to hear it. And unless he's ready to tell it,
getting the full truth can be a thorny matter.

So Help Me God!

If your husband came to you with a confession as a first step toward getting real and
seeking recovery, he is apt to be more willing to talk. If you found out another way, and
you come to him with an accusation, expecting him to respond with an admission of

guilt and give you more information, you will be more likely to have an experience akin to pulling teeth.

In our experience, husbands commonly offer a "sampler confession." In confessing something small, a man may be testing the waters to see how the truth is received, or he may delude himself into thinking that as long as he tells *some* truth, he is telling *the* truth.

Telling the full truth can be excruciatingly painful to a man, and facing how much sin he's been carrying around can seem unbearable. Forming it all into words and letting them out where they can't be put back into hiding can feel like the beginning of the end. If a man still cares about his family, he's bound by the fear that the information will be the end of his marriage, his rights to see his children, and his entire world as he knows it—not to mention the end of his secret coping mechanism.

> Problems far too big for me to solve are piled higher than my head. Meanwhile my sins, too many to count, have all caught up with me and I am ashamed to look up. My heart quails within me. (Psalm 40:12)

Given all the reasons to hide, getting to the truth frequently involves unwrapping a few more lies—"But I've already told you everything," "That's all I remember," "It only happened the two times." This is why it's critical that you build up some strong support *before* you go in demanding the whole truth.

> He who loves wisdom loves his own best interest and will be a success. (Proverbs 19:8)

What's Love Got to Do with It?

> Direct me in the path of your commands, for there I find delight. Turn my heart toward your statutes and not toward selfish gain. (Psalm 119:35–36, NIV)

In "Anyway," a popular song by Martina McBride, she says we can build something for years only to have one storm destroy all our work. "Build it anyway," she sings. And we can love someone who may choose to leave. "Love 'em anyway."

Anyway

McBride's song swims against the current of popular music, defining love not as a feeling but as the basis for a life lived to the fullest. This is the love required in marriage. We risk being hurt when we're pursuing love the way God defines love. Being "in love" or "falling out of love" does not express the true nature of this deeply misunderstood foundation of life. Love isn't a feeling or even an emotion. It is a foundation of life.

Love phrases like these get tossed around frequently:

- "I'm falling in love."
- "Let's make love."
- "He only loves me when it's convenient."
- "Just love him through it."
- "I don't feel love for him anymore."

Yet while romantic love can be lovely, the love God wants us to have for our spouses is:

- desiring what's best for them
- putting their needs before our own
- desiring God's will for them
- actively caring for them
- a decision of the will to sacrifice

The love God gives us for others is called *agape* (uh-GAH-pay) in Greek. It is voluntary and unconditional. Our common understanding of love is primarily emotional and sentimental, so we easily confuse loving our husbands with how we feel toward them, when love is actually how we *behave* toward them. Your husband's needs are different now, but some loving actions include:

- drawing new boundaries
- speaking the truth about your marriage
- withdrawing sexually
- being kind when you are feeling hateful
- letting him see your hurt and anger
- separating from him
- allowing him to suffer the natural consequences of his behavior
- praying for him

- involving trusted friends to come alongside your husband
- locating a support group and other resources for your husband

Obviously, there are more ways, but exercising this kind of love when you're angry or hurt can either feel like the opposite of love or opposed to the spiteful feelings stirring inside. Loving as your husband needs to be loved won't always feel good. In fact, if you've been one to gauge love based upon your feelings, you may even feel you're being a bad person when you try to love this way. Romans 12:9 says, "Don't just pretend that you love others: really love them. Hate what is wrong. Stand on the side of the good."

If you expect to love your husband this way, you'll need to remember that your husband's fear is what got him into this mess in the first place. If it takes him weeks or even months to start telling you the whole truth, be purposeful about not condemning him for not being more truthful sooner. You both are weighing issues of trust; you are looking for his truthfulness, and he is looking for safety in telling the truth.

How Sweet It Is to Be Loved by You

Consider God's instruction on loving in relationship: it always starts with Him. A teacher of religion once asked Jesus, " 'Of all the commandments, which is the most important?' Jesus replied, 'The one that says,... "The Lord our God is the one and only God. And you must love him with all your heart and soul and mind and strength." The second is: "You must love others as much as yourself." No other commandments are greater than these' " (Mark 12:28–31).

Jesus gave priority to loving God because, in God's design of the world, loving Him first creates the foundation upon which our lives work best. When we love God first, obeying the other nine commandments naturally follows. Listening for His opinion about our circumstances, obeying Him moment by moment, and adjusting ourselves to what we know He desires of us keeps us from making decisions that may look right from our perspective but can actually lead to harm.

Of course, it's easier to do what pleases *us*. However, if we keep our focus on loving God first (and how He loved us first), we will find ourselves loving others as they need to be loved. This is the key to responding to the whole truth in a positive, redemptive way for your marriage.

As I said, this kind of love can cause discomfort. It may even appear you're moving further away from what you want. But God's commandment to love Him first is a two-way street, and He travels with you all the way. Why? Because He loves you more than you can ever know, and He wants what's best for you—each of you. He has the long view of your life and knows what you need to become the person He intended. Everything He asks of you is asked out of love, including the things He's asking of you now. And when you know God has your best interests at heart, you can surrender the controls to Him.

Sometimes It's Hard to Be a Woman

Does all this mean I'm supposed to overlook my husband's sin and just 'love him through it?' Isn't that codependence? Real love doesn't overlook evil. When the motivating force is love, you can extend:

- *compassion* without taking undue responsibility for his behavior
- *humility* without accepting domination or control
- *grace* without removing the natural consequences of his actions
- *helpfulness* without causing him to rely on you unjustly

When motivated by godly love, these qualities are empowering and life giving. They do require a person to work at them, to sacrifice, practice endurance, and receive strength from outside support. And to be sure, these are *not* popular characteristics in our day and age. But if you've made the choice—the healing choice—you are not just another damaged wife: you're preparing for the marriage marathon. In a way, facing the whole truth with your husband is potentially the greatest personal training in godly love you will ever receive.

And you can be sure there is a prize for everyone who endures to the finish.

Choosing this path does not minimize the sin. You can always take a strong stand against sin. Be firm in your values. But beyond this temporary difficult journey, you can finally learn to address sin with love, in humility and compassion, being helpful and decisive about giving grace, while repairing the damage and seeking full repentance. Consider these scriptures:

On Love

Though we have never yet seen God, when we love each other God lives in us and his love within us grows ever stronger. (1 John 4:12)

On Compassion

Be kind to each other, tenderhearted, forgiving one another, just as God has forgiven you because you belong to Christ. (Ephesians 4:32)

On Humility and Helpfulness

If a Christian is overcome by some sin, you who are godly should gently and humbly help him back onto the right path, remembering that next time it might be one of you who is in the wrong. (Galatians 6:1)

On Grace

Don't you realize how patient he is being with you?… Can't you see that he has been waiting all this time without punishing you, to give you time to turn from your sin? His kindness is meant to lead you to repentance. (Romans 2:4)

In previous chapters, I talked about taking a hard stand against sin. Yet in these verses, we see that the loving response can look much like the opposite. When we love the sinner, we don't stop hating the sin; we're merely giving truth its proper context. Truth wrapped in love looks like grace. This is the only way to encourage people to risk coming out of isolation and into intimate relationship. You might think of it this way:

If we're to honor both our [helper role and submissive role] as wives, balanced accountability must always arise from these two cornerstones:

1. My marriage is not all about me.

2. When I hold him accountable, my focus must be on my choices as well as his.

Christ's broader view of marriage prevented pain from dominating my heart and kept Fred's pain on my mind, enabling me to consider mercy and patience, regardless of the sin involved.

You need that broader view too. Sure, his sin is betraying and crushing you, but it is also revealing his deeper wounds and addictions below the surface. He's not just a straying husband but a brother lost in the futility of his thinking and now corrupted by his deceitful desires. It's not just about you.

The way I came to view things, I was not just Fred's wife, called to respectfully submit to his leadership and to always be ravished in his arms. I was *also* his good Samaritan, compelled by my love to dress his wounds, and *also* his friend, taking on the "iron sharpens iron" role described in Proverbs 27:17.

That dual picture of applying the dressing and grinding the iron portrays our helper role pretty well. When we make sure to include that mental picture of applying dressings to our husband's wounds, our primary focus remains on our own choices in the situation, rather than on our husbands'. (*Every Heart Restored*, 157–58)

Grace, defined as "undeserved favor," is a form of unconditional acceptance that can't be earned. It is the catalyst that inspires people to change because of the love they encounter.

Operating in both truth and love—applying both the iron and the dressings—is the life Jesus calls us to. Recall Jesus's encounter with the adulterous woman when no one remained to throw the first stone at her (see John 8:1–11):

"Where are your accusers? Didn't even one of them condemn you?"

"No, sir," she said.

And Jesus said, "Neither do I. Go and sin no more."

Grace does not deny truth. It offers forgiveness but challenges you to a changed life. As the one who has been sinned against, you may be tempted to throw stones at your husband. Maybe you already have. Yes, that brings a temporary satisfaction, to be sure. But doing so can do nothing to improve your situation or your future. There is another way.

Just as Jesus directed the stone throwers to examine themselves, you must choose to examine your own life and consider how flawless and sinless *you* have been. Are you cleared to start stoning him? Imagine if what Jesus was writing in the sand were your own sins. Would you have stuck around to throw stones at the adulterer?

Smoke Gets in Your Eyes

Pride is the underlying attitude that blinds us to our own faults. God calls you to help your husband, but what that help looks like may be different than you expect. If you are operating out of pride rather than humility, you won't have the insight or the strength to blend truth and love.

This one characteristic, pride, leads to another: judging. The two are joined at the hip, and Jesus addressed it in Matthew: "Do not judge, or you too will be judged.... Why do you look at the speck of sawdust in your brother's eye and pay no attention to the plank in your own eye?... You hypocrite, first take the plank out of your own eye, and then you will see clearly to remove the speck from your brother's eye" (7:1, 3, 5, NIV). Jesus does not forbid consequences for wrongdoing. But the notion that we can judge others objectively overlooks the fact that we are not the supreme judge of sin. Extending love and grace toward your husband requires remembering that none of us is without sin. When we're seeing that clearly, we can help our brother in love.

Take this opportunity to eradicate pride from your life in order to help your husband take the courageous actions required of him now. One woman, Alicia, is a good example for us:

> My husband and I have been scuffling over his sexual sin for over a year now after seven years of his lies were exposed. Recently, however, I've changed my approach. I've been working on understanding his battle and how hard it is in the world today to stay pure, and I have also looked at myself in the mirror and seen some things I don't like, so I've even asked God to help me in my own struggle to trust again. In the process, I've truly given this all to God, and I feel as if a weight has lifted.
>
> The truth is, in my anger I had been holding back from my husband in many ways so as to not get hurt again, but in my holding back I saw the pain in his eyes whenever he made big strides in his battle and I'd just dismiss the gains, telling him it would just be a matter of time before he hurt me again. Whenever he *did* stumble again, I would be downright mean to him.

We've had several talks in the last few months, though, and our church has been teaching us about discipleship and what that really means between Christians. My husband and I made a new commitment to apply two lessons of discipleship to our relationship together, to *keep moving forward* and to remember that *without failure, there can be no success.* From now on, I choose to see his failure for what it is, just part of his growth as a disciple of Christ, and I'm going to keep moving forward together with him. With this new commitment to God and to my husband, I feel more positive than I have since all this began. My husband has made a promise to God and to me that he will not quit until he's the example that God wants him to be to me and our kids. That promise wasn't good enough for me early on, but, gratefully, my arrogance and pride isn't what it used to be either.

MY · STONE · WORK

Insight

Consider the things you've done in the past that have required God's forgiveness. Remember the feelings surrounding the events, any fear you felt before being forgiven, and the surprising relief after you were forgiven.

Use these memories to deliver a death blow to your pride. How can those recollections help you develop compassion toward your husband? Journal the steps you need to take to strike out pride, and write what you feel called to do to act in greater compassion.

Action

Make the decision to act on your journaled thoughts. Do not wait. Share them with your walking companion, and ask her to hold you accountable to respond against condemnation and for truth and love.

These Boots Are Made for Walking

Remember, hard hearts are the secret killer of relationships. How you handle your husband's failures, sins, and weaknesses will determine in large part your ability to survive this betrayal. When we harden our hearts, we say no to the possibility of reconciliation, redemption, repentance, and growth. A hardened heart isn't willing to wait and see. It has closed the door and walked away.

The Bible places a high value on tenderheartedness. God allows divorce because a marriage can't survive a hardened heart. It breaks God's heart to see a marriage destroyed because of a hardened heart. This is not His plan. Marriage is intended to be the union of two forgivers. If your husband has hardened his heart to his sin, the marriage cannot heal until he changes. But if he has demonstrated repentance, humbled himself, and sought forgiveness, he has shown that he has changed—his heart has become tender.

If you're strapping up your boots to walk away in spite of his changed heart, consider your motive. God gives spouses permission to divorce if there has been infidelity. But if we decide to leave after a husband has truly changed, we risk bringing condemnation down not only on him but on ourselves as well.

With God, all things are possible. He can wipe away sin and heal a broken heart. He can renew and heal your marriage. But He gives us the freedom to choose the path we will take.

MY · STONE · WORK

Insight

Study 1 Corinthians 13 carefully. Write what you think each attribute might look like in your present circumstance. Focus on the condition of your heart as you seek answers.

Start preparing your heart to love your husband with God's love instead of the conditional kind of love most of the world offers. What are the loving actions

God is calling you to take to restore your marriage? to respond to your husband's sin? to demonstrate and grow in grace? to better understand the forgiveness you've been shown? to finally understand the fears your husband has lived with for years?

Action

Your insights are your action points for the next leg of your journey. Put your heart, mind, and feet into gear to carry them out. Share your insights with your walking companion. Ask for accountability with your attitudes and actions.

Just Give Me Some Truth

So once you are certain of your loving foundation, how do you encourage him to tell you the whole truth? When you feel emotionally ready, you do need to know the rest. Give him the opportunity, and if he is not ready to share more or denies there is more, agree to talk about it a few days later when you are both emotionally prepared. But don't badger.

If you're willing to work on the marriage, offer that, but you do not need to be the strong one. These points of major disclosure are gut-wrenching, and emotions have a profound physical impact on the body. Expect to be exhausted after a devastating disclosure, possibly for many days.

If he is at a point of surrender and is willing to be honest, you likely have an inexhaustible list of questions for him. But be cautious. You do *not* need to know all the whos, whats, wheres, whens, and hows. While there is reasonable information that you must acquire to make sense of the lies and missing pieces, you do not necessarily need or want details about specific encounters or graphic information. Resist the urge to dig for what he liked doing. You don't want to be left with images that could cause more damage to your heart. There's wisdom in not asking how you compared or the myriad other such details. This is not what needs to be discussed, and there is never cause to dwell on sin, which is what you would be tempted to do if you had this information.

MY · STONE · WORK

Insight

Whether your husband is ready to confess or not, determine to prepare yourself to express love, humility, and compassion in the course of getting the whole truth. Pray and meditate on the scriptures in this chapter as well as your own need for and experience of forgiveness.

When you're ready to hear his confession, you will know it.

Action

1. If you are certain in your heart that you are willing to go God's way regardless of your husband's sins, you may express that to your husband. Let him know that while you can't guarantee an absence of anger and tears, you are willing to hear the truth about his behavior and face the work of restoration ahead. If you like, tell him you have made a commitment to love in spite of how you feel at the moment. This can be an important step in demonstrating real love and creating an atmosphere of security in which your husband can share.

2. Make sure you are specific with your husband about what kind of information you want him to tell and what should be left out. Clarify that you want to know, for example, every general type of behavior he acts out with (such as masturbation, Internet porn, sex shows, live chats, prostitutes, and so on). Have him confess when and where he typically engages in the specific behaviors.

3. Specifics that are difficult but prudent to know involve people in your day-to-day life, such as friends, neighbors, co-workers, and employees. This information will be important in establishing healthy boundaries and eliminating certain situations and relationships.

4. Though he may feel as though he is under a microscope, it's best if all the truth that you need to know gets out on the table in a condensed time frame. This is for your benefit, but be aware that if your husband is not entirely ready to talk, he may not be telling the whole truth. As he becomes more convinced of your sincerity and his safety, the truth may win out. The downside for you will be experiencing fresh pain about each new revelation when he musters the courage to get real.

5. When you hear his confession, you may still feel betrayed and angry. Those emotions are valid. You clearly know, because of your sense of justice, that you were wronged, but if your focus is ultimately on following God's promptings to make decisions, you will be anchored to the Rock; your emotions won't be guiding you down desperate or destructive trails.

6. Ask him to commit to never telling anyone anything more about the sexual involvements than he's told you. Ask him to make his full confession to someone in his group. If he isn't in a group, encourage him to join or start one with the information provided at the end of this chapter.

7. During these times, determine not to share anything with him about circumstances in your life that have been directly affected by his actions. This may be extremely difficult, but as we discussed earlier in chapter 2, keep an ongoing "loss list" in your journal, detailing those things that come to mind as you walk through this rock-riddled road together. How might he feel, in time, about all the justifiable hurt you could have unloaded on him at a very vulnerable time but didn't? There will be a time on the journey ahead when he is able to see what his actions have cost you. Seek his best interests and those of the marriage, and you will be rewarded.

Finally, remember not to make any rash decisions during this time. In due season, your sense of perspective on these intense events will likely evolve.

My Prayer for Responding to Truth in Love

Lord, I seek the truth. Give me Your perfect wisdom to guide me, and show me how to love him with Your love, even when he seems unlovable. Give me unwavering determination to do the loving things You call me to do and to control my emotions and reject any pride in my heart. Show me my imperfection covered by Your grace, and show me what love looks like, how to hope in the liberation of truth, and how to guard my soul from unnecessary pain. Remind me, Lord, that my husband's sins are not a reflection of my shortcomings but his own need for Your love and grace. In Jesus Christ's name, amen.

To obtain resources and information about finding a group in his area, contact Avenue at our Web site, AvenueResource.com, or by calling our toll-free help line at 877-326-7000.

Eleventh Landmark

Decisions: Stay or Divorce

You are my hiding place from every storm of life; you even
keep me from getting into trouble! You surround me with
songs of victory. I will instruct you (says the Lord) and
guide you along the best pathway for your life; I will advise
you and watch your progress.

PSALM 32:7–8

What do you do now that you know the truth? There will be decisions to make, but
the early months after discovering your husband's betrayal are not the time to make
life-altering decisions. There is just too much to process. Often during the early
months, a woman feels pressured by her husband or family to make a "forever" decision, either to stay married or get divorced. Many women feel they must make up their
minds right away or forever hold their peace. Some also feel they'll be trapped in the
marriage if they don't take their chance to bail out immediately.

You have the right, indeed the responsibility, to take your time. For some women,
the immediate reaction is to run…and fast. Wanting to bail out is understandable, and
that feeling can stem from distrust, anger, jealousy, or wounded pride. But running
away frequently leads to greater hurt; many mistakes are made in the heat of emotion.

So right now, give yourself permission to take some time before making your permanent decision. My best advice is to allow approximately six months for your emotions to settle down and to process and adjust to your "new normal."

Staying

Staying married should be a point of personal decision, a choice one freely and deliberately chooses to make. It should never be chosen to preserve the status quo or to take the path of least resistance. If your husband has admitted betrayal and sought forgiveness, the decision to stay is a courageous one. When both partners are committed not just to stay, but to renew, grow, and strengthen their marriage, God's plan for a lifelong union is honored: "A man should leave his father and mother, and be forever united to his wife. The two shall become one—no longer two, but one! And no man may divorce what God has joined together" (Matthew 19:5–6).

Although Jesus allowed divorce for the crime of adultery, He didn't recommend it. On the contrary, He insisted that divorce disrupts God's plan for marriage. He left the way open for repentance and forgiveness, even in the case of sexual sin and other sins against a spouse and the marital union.

If your marriage vows have been broken, they need to be renegotiated. This is a good time to ask yourself, *Under what conditions would I choose to stay married?* Even if your response is, *No matter what, I'm in it forever,* make that a positive decision, not a victim's resignation. To just stay married because "the Lord…hates divorce" (Malachi 2:16) may be regarded by some as a righteous stand, but I see it used by women as an excuse to avoid reality or change and not take responsibility for their lives. It is never Christlike to idly endure evil as a martyr or a victim, enabling a husband to continue in his sin.

Deciding whether to remain married calls for careful consideration of this question: what will be the best situation for everyone involved? Family stability, emotional trauma, and financial concerns should all factor in to your decision, but none should carry more weight than what God is telling you in your time with Him.

When I came to this point of crisis in my marriage, I decided I wanted to know God's personal view of my marriage and life. I knew what the Bible said, but I wanted God to personalize it for me, to speak to me individually. I knew there would be no condemnation if I left, but I was fairly new to the idea of allowing Him in on all my decisions in life. I had made some very poor and costly choices without His wisdom in the past.

If you are willing to let God work through you, miracles do happen. With repentance, hardened hearts can be softened, and broken hearts can be restored.

Above all, give yourself grace in this decision. Don't expect to figure it all out in just a few weeks. You're going through much emotional trauma and turmoil, and you need time to process and regain your balance and perspective. The best thing to do during this time is to pray. And as you do, watch your husband's behavior, seek the truth in love, work at remaining open to God's opinion through consistent time spent with Him, and obtain counsel with your walking companion, group, pastor and/or counselor.

And when you do finally decide, make sure it's *your* decision.

Divorce

If your vows have been broken by adultery, God will release you from them if you so choose. He does not say you must go, nor does He say you must stay. In fact, He gives you freedom from the law by allowing remarriage for people whose covenantal vows were broken by their spouses. "I tell you this, that anyone who divorces [his or her spouse], except for fornication, and marries another, commits adultery" (Matthew 19:9).

However, the decision to divorce is definitely an important one. I have known women to make an immediate decision to divorce upon discovery of their husband's infidelity. Although this may be where you end up eventually, I believe that this early stage is not the time to make that momentous decision. In fact, I believe the best decision for the time is to "decide to decide" in six months. Above all else, don't decide your future—and your children's future—based on emotions that are changing day by day, hour by hour, or moment by moment, for that matter.

How do you make such a decision? The same way you choose whether to stay. Pray. Watch your husband's behavior. Seek God's opinion. Get wise counsel, and talk with your walking companion. Then make it your decision, because ultimately it will become the life you will live.

Know that God doesn't hate divorced people. He hates adultery and divorce because of what it does to people.

This is another thing you do. You drown the Lord's altar with tears, weeping and wailing because he no longer accepts the offerings you bring him. You ask why he no longer accepts them. It is because he knows you have broken your promise to the wife you married when you were young. She was your partner, and you have broken your promise to her, although you promised before God that you would be faithful to her. Didn't God make you one body and spirit with her? What was his purpose in this? It was that you should have children who are truly God's people. So make sure that none of you breaks his promise to his wife. "I hate divorce," says the Lord God of Israel. "I hate it when one of you does such a cruel thing to his wife. Make sure that you do not break your promise to be faithful to your wife." (Malachi 2:13–16, GNT)

God knows how much we are hurt by betrayal of vows and divorce. But know that you will not escape your current pain by means of divorce. Divorce is not a cure-all for the turmoil you are experiencing. It's not a shortcut past grief, anger, bitterness, or forgiveness. Neither is it a remedy for a broken heart.

Children of divorce live the rest of their lives with the debris of a broken home. Recent studies on the detrimental effect that divorce has on children are difficult to dispute. Know that you have challenges ahead of you either way. They will be a different set of challenges from those you encountered in your marriage, neither is arguably easier than the other. Ask God to search your heart and your motives. It may help to ask a key question: what are you leaving behind and what are you moving toward? Knowing the importance God places on marriage, it's clear that divorce should be the last resort, only considered after you've pursued every other option. As I wrote in *The Healing Choice:*

Wouldn't it be a great package deal if we could divorce the hurt and hatred at the same time we leave the marriage? I have learned from personal experience that divorce is not an all-inclusive, final deal. In legal terms, divorce has finality, but in the emotional, spiritual, and physical realms, it has no end. You can't divorce your emotions. You may wrestle with your religious belief on the issue; you'll probably have a new financial status. You'll face practical and emotional issues involving some or all of the following: children, in-laws, mutual friends, and your ex and his new mate. These issues may have to be navigated for the rest of your life. If you desire to build a new life after divorce on a foundation of emotional, physical, and spiritual health, you will have a healing process to journey through.

Consider the option of divorce, but recognize the burden this dramatic step carries with it. The *process* for making this decision should be as weighty as the decision itself. " 'Everything is permissible'—but not everything is constructive. Nobody should seek his own good, but the good of others" (1 Corinthians 10:23–24, NIV). It would be easy for abused wives to misinterpret that verse and use it as an excuse not to take the action she needs to end living with abuse. But examine your heart and consider your motives—whether there is any pride or unwillingness to forgive—and know that those attitudes are as disdainful as infidelity to God. And if you're seriously considering the divorce option, seek out support and accountability before acting.

It's no walk in the park, but it's worth waiting to determine if your husband is repentant and surrendered to going God's way. The waiting, praying, and doing what God whispers to your heart may seem like putting your life on hold forever. But this waiting time will pass, and it will be worth it. Remember, your future and your children's future is at stake. If you allow yourself adequate time to make a well-examined decision, you won't regret it.

May my spoken words and unspoken thoughts be pleasing even to you, O Lord my Rock and my Redeemer. (Psalm 19:14)

In the next chapter, we'll delve into a third option, somewhere between staying and divorcing.

MY • STONE • WORK

Insight

What stones do you need to look under as you make your decision? Is your fear of being alone a rock that will trip you up? Or is bitterness making your decision for you? Just sit and ponder for a bit. Write down every thought that swirls through your mind concerning your desire to leave or stay. It doesn't matter if your thoughts are rational, emotional, calculating, or spiritual. Just chronicle them.

Action

Now isn't the time to take actions that will determine your future. This is one time when the action called for is *stillness*. Regardless of what that list you wrote says, just let it be…for now. Six months may seem like a long time—and it's not a dictate from the Bible. But it's a reasonable amount of time to give yourself before choosing. I've known women who began reconciliation with their husbands within weeks and others who waited years. While you're in the wait-and-see process, complete all the stone work sections and explore the suggested assignments. They will help you make this decision. Look at the insights you wrote during this stone work exercise over the course of several months, and consider what things have changed and what has remained the same.

· · · · · · · · · · · · ❁ · · · · · · · · · · · ·

My Prayer for Wise Decisions

Lord, help me to choose wisely, for I know my choices now may even affect the eternal destiny of some. Reveal to me Your thoughts and Your will for my path, Help me not be hasty or seek my own desires. Protect me and my family in our step forward in faith, seeking to do Your will. Let my decisions and my actions bring my husband closer to You and the healing You offer. In Jesus's name, amen.

· ·

Twelfth Landmark

Deciding on Separation

He shows how to distinguish right from wrong, how to find
the right decision every time. For wisdom and truth will
enter the very center of your being, filling your life with joy.
You will be given the sense to stay away from evil men who
want you to be their partners in crime—men who turn from
God's ways to walk down dark and evil paths, and exult in
doing wrong, for they thoroughly enjoy their sins.... Follow
the steps of the godly instead, and stay on the right path.

PROVERBS 2:9–14, 20

Under stress, we often tend toward a black-and-white way of thinking that staying married or divorcing are our only two choices. But there is another choice—separation—which is often misunderstood, underutilized, and poorly implemented.

People frequently want to separate for misguided reasons:

- *I can get a feel for what it would be like to be divorced.*
- *This might be a good punishment for him.*
- *Maybe I could date others and make him jealous.*

Better than these poor motivations are motives based on biblical principles:

- *Removing the offender:* "I will sing about your loving-kindness and your justice, Lord. I will sing your praises! I will try to walk a blameless path, but how I need your help, especially in my own home, where I long to act as I should.

Help me to refuse the low and vulgar things; help me to abhor all crooked deals of every kind, to have no part in them. I will reject all selfishness and stay away from every evil.... I will not allow those who deceive and lie to stay in my house" (Psalm 101:1–4, 7).

- *Repentance of the offender:* "I run in the path of your commands, for you have set my heart free. Teach me, O LORD, to follow your decrees; then I will keep them to the end. Give me understanding, and I will keep your law and obey it with all my heart. Direct me in the path of your commands, for there I find delight. Turn my heart toward your statutes and not toward selfish gain. Turn my eyes away from worthless things; preserve my life according to your word" (Psalm 119:32–37, NIV).
- *Reconciliation with the offender:* "You have become living building-stones for God's use in building his house. What's more, you are his holy priests; so come to him—[you who are acceptable to him because of Jesus Christ]—and offer to God those things that please him" (1 Peter 2:5).

Other benefits interwoven with these three principles are:

- creating distance to regain peace, wisdom, and safety
- gaining objectivity to evaluate motives and behavior
- creating the motivation in the offender to change
- making a definitive commitment to the good of the relationship

In this chapter we'll deal with the three distinct processes of separation which correspond to the three Rs above:

- How do you remove the offender?
- How do you measure change and repentance?
- When, if ever, should you reconcile?

The Case for Separation

Carol has confronted Brad about his behavior, but there has been no change. She has gone to a counselor with Brad. No change. She has prayed relentlessly that he would change, but he has not. She has sought their pastor's help. Brad declined the pastor's encouragement to join a men's group. Carol has set firm boundaries and even warned him that she's considering separation.

Brad says he wants to stay married and doesn't want to separate, but he clearly doesn't want to make any real, sincere efforts to change his behavior. Carol has asked Brad to leave. Brad finally moves out at Carol's insistence.

Carol has prayed for Brad and her marriage for years but recognizes that she's at a crossroads, having used up all the tools available. Because she is still willing to work toward healing their marriage, she decides to separate to (1) remove herself from Brad's deception, betrayal, and lack of repentance, and (2) to wake him up to his poor choices. She hopes he'll repent and that there will be a full reconciliation of the marriage. But she's waiting to see.

The desired outcome here is that Brad would finally see his sin, repent, make a decision to change, and do the work of facing his deeper issues. If Brad truly wants to save his marriage, he will face his denial and take the steps to quit his old lifestyle. Finally, he will acknowledge the destruction he's caused and seek restoration with God and Carol and his children.

This is the ideal outcome that well-purposed separation can bring about. It can, and does, happen. There are no guarantees, of course, but Carol knew she needed distance to see if Brad would experience a true heart change after so many other attempts had failed.

The Example of Hosea

We can also look to the prophet Hosea for a godly view of separation. The story goes that God asked Hosea to marry a prostitute named Gomer to illustrate His people's unfaithfulness and His offer for reconciliation. When Gomer betrayed Hosea, God spoke words to Hosea illuminating the covenant He had made with His people:

> I am no longer her husband. Beg her to stop her harlotry, to quit giving herself to others. If she doesn't, I will strip her as naked as the day she was born, and cause her to waste away and die of thirst as in a land riddled with famine and drought. And I will not give special favors to her children as I would to my own, for they are not my children; they belong to other men.
>
> For [she] has committed adultery. She did a shameful thing when she said, "I'll run after other men and sell myself to them for food and drinks and clothes." (Hosea 2:2–5)

Do you hear how angry Hosea sounds? Anyone who suggests we should put on a happy face and quietly bear the burden of infidelity in secret is deceived. Hosea's reaction was directed by God to make Gomer and all His people feel the consequences of their behavior. And Hosea did take her back, but only under certain conditions:

I will fence her in with briars and thornbushes; I'll block the road before her to make her lose her way, so that when she runs after her lovers she will not catch up with them. She will search for them but not find them. Then she will think, "I might as well return to my husband, for I was better off with him than I am now." (Hosea 2:6–7)

For some women, this kind of interference might be confused with codependent actions. But God is showing how He deals with us, how He gets our attention and encourages us to come back to Him.

You may already be making it easy for your husband to continue his behavior. If you know he's having an affair, he should not be living with you. If he has a porn addiction, cut off your Internet service. If he's spending money on prostitutes or live sex shows, cut off his funds and credit cards. "I will put an end to all her joys, her parties, holidays, and feasts" (Hosea 2:11).

When you're separated, limiting access to resources, his children, and the house is a reasonable, biblical method to protect yourself and make him face his sin. As the story of Hosea shows, the desired outcome is to force the adulterer to realize she is better off in the marriage.

Hosea uncovers Gomer's sin: "Now I will expose her nakedness in public for all her lovers to see, and no one will be able to rescue her from my hand" (Hosea 2:10). Once you recognize what he's been doing behind your back, you need to prayerfully decide who should know the truth about your husband's behavior. Revealing his sin is a biblical step, not to shame him, but to make him face his actions and, hopefully, repent.

Once Hosea recognizes a surrendered spirit, he pursues Gomer once again: "But I will court her again, and bring her into the wilderness, and speak to her tenderly there. There I will…transform her Valley of Troubles into a Door of Hope. She will respond to me there, singing with joy as in days long ago in her youth." (Hosea 2:14–15).

Hosea arranged for Gomer to live nearby, waiting for proof that she had stopped her adulterous ways before trusting her and reconciling their marriage. Though it's next to impossible to fathom the humility it took for him to do this, with God's help, Hosea's pride took a backseat. Though we can also understand this chapter of Hosea as God's message to the people of Israel, it's plain to see that God wants us, when separating from a spouse, to consider forgiveness and reconciliation from His perspective of tender strength and unconditional love.

A Mandate for Separation

Have nothing to do with the fruitless deeds of darkness, but rather expose them. (Ephesians 5:11, NIV)

This verse states the responsibility plainly: we're not to be companions to those who choose to live lives of sin. As difficult as it may be, we must distance ourselves and reveal their errors. This instruction becomes urgent in the case of physical abuse—an abused woman must remove such danger from her home. The same applies in cases of emotional abuse where the home is in turmoil due to the husband's selfishness or unrepentant attitude. If you don't trust him with your children, or even if you just need space to deal with your emotions, you may not wish to share a roof with your betrayer right now. But remember, it's not a punishment but a consequence of his actions, intended to help him break through his own denial and face the fallout of his choices.

The best arrangement is for the husband to leave at the wife's request. If, however, he is unwilling to leave or is dangerous, the wife's other choice would be to leave with her children. In the following section, we'll cover these various situations.

The Separation Plan (Nonviolent Husband)

Your husband's willingness to cooperate with a separation will often determine how the process should proceed.

If he takes responsibility for his actions, finds suitable housing for himself for the duration of the separation, and is willing to provide for you and the children, that's the first step accomplished. If he is unwilling to leave, but you have determined it is not in the best interests of you and your children to stay, you'll need to determine a plan for departing. Seek wise counsel from God and others at every step. If your husband is unwilling to support you financially, know that God is in this for your mutual healing. There is a way.

Here are some important considerations to make prior to a separation.

Decide Where to Live

- Assess every option about where to live, and make sure your final choice is reasonable for an indefinite term. You don't want to back yourself into a corner and return home prematurely because you don't know where to go. While renting a small apartment is the simplest way to go, limited finances may make this option impossible. If that's the case, start by making a list of every person or family who would probably welcome you into their homes. If you have a job location and the children's school to consider, start by focusing your list on those geographic needs. Then start calling. You'll obviously have to explain the circumstances if the person isn't already aware of your marital issues. If you're speaking to mutual friends or family members, let them know you aren't asking anyone to take sides; in fact, you're hoping to restore what's broken.

- It is encouraging to have a family member offer to house you for as long as it takes. This situation will probably feel the most familiar, comfortable, and stable for your children. But even if you have that "luxury" and can't see what could go wrong, develop a backup plan. To avoid being an unnecessary burden to any one person or couple, consider seeking two or more friends who can each house you for a month or two at a time.

- A few other ideas for housing from real-life experiences: One woman moved into one of the rental apartments she and her husband owned when it became vacant (and changed the locks). Another woman lived in her parents' motor home, which they kept parked in their long driveway. Another moved into her own home's pool house. A woman moved into a friend's tiny guest cottage. A woman without children made do quite creatively: she owned her own business and organized and partitioned a small space for a twin bed and clothing in the storage room. She went to her gym each morning for not only a workout, but a complete shower and grooming as well. For meals she ate out frugally and also used the small fridge, microwave, and coffee maker that were already in her place of business. One mother moved in with another divorced mother, and their job schedules were such that they took turns watching the children and shared household expenses.

- The children should not be used as pawns. Attempt to plan with your husband for his time together with the children. If there is lack of cooperation or if his response escalates into anger, it would be prudent prior to separation to seek legal counsel about establishing temporary custody.

Determine How You Will Pay Your Expenses

- If you are unfamiliar with your household finances and accounts because this has been your husband's role, this is the time to get educated. Let me state in advance that this is not snooping; it's taking responsibility for yourself. While he is away, go through the household bookkeeping system to find all checking and savings accounts, and determine what the account balances are. Find out which credit cards are in both your names. Do you have an equity line of credit? There is much more information that is important to learn, but for now, the focus is on liquid assets and available credit.

- It may be prudent to consult with a Christian accountant or attorney for the purpose of protecting your assets and keeping your husband from incurring new debt in your name. He or she can give you the particulars on the legal protection you can put in place. Remember, you are only going down this avenue because your husband is uncooperative and unwilling to change.

- While it would be inappropriate to drain all the family assets, you will need money to cover your own expenses, such as food, toiletries, and gas. This is a delicate issue if funds are limited. But if you leave the majority of the money for your husband, how do you know he'll only use it for necessities? This issue, too, could benefit from the insight of a wise friend, attorney, or accountant. Just be careful not to get sucked into the bottomless pit of attorney counsel. Some cities have inexpensive paralegal services or even free legal aid worth looking into.

- If you are unable to take reasonable funds from the family account and do not hold a paying job, consider what skills you have and how you can juggle your schedule with your children in order to hold down a job.

Decide What to Take with You

- Two words: travel light. Take versatile, season-stretching, wrinkle-free clothing you own, both for you and your children. Of course, bring things that are expensive to buy again, such as a warm coat. Bring all the personal toiletries you need—regular size, not travel size. This isn't a week's vacation. Bring your favorite sleeping pillows. Bring your trusty Bible, maybe a sentimental treasure, and a family photo. Have your children pick their favorite few things to keep with them.

- If you are in tight quarters, sharing space with other families, consider renting a *small* self-storage space. It will provide you a space to store more clothes and keep business supplies and other things unique to your circumstances. Just don't fill it with needless stuff. Make this space a personal closet where you can easily retrieve things. Put clothes on a portable hanging rack instead of stuffed in boxes, and find cheap shelving at a garage sale. Otherwise, everything will be on the floor, or you'll be climbing over stacks of boxes to find things.

- If you are furnishing your own place, take what you can from your family home without leaving it bare. Consider taking the seldom-used living room sofa, guest bed, and so on. Take some everyday dishware and kitchen supplies, as most kitchens have more than enough to supply two homes.

- Make lists of what you will need to take. On a day your husband will not be around, do your banking early in the morning, and then pack and make a precise exit, so that you don't need to come back for more things. It would be helpful to have two friends to help you load and transport your things. As you can see, you will be faced with a lifestyle adjustment. Prepare yourself mentally and spiritually to stay the course. It's when the going gets tough that one gets weary in the going. Don't choose compromise for comfort. Hopefully, the end will be worth the means to get where you want to be—back home.

We should make plans—counting on God to direct us. (Proverbs 16:9)

Separation from a Violent Husband

It's a fact. The use of pornography increases the incidence of family violence. Whether it's physical or emotional, whether it's directed at you, your children, or even someone else, you need to seek refuge from abuse. Enlist the help of a friend if you can to give you courage to set a solid plan and enact it. You must not allow the abuse to continue. As the Bible says, "A hot-tempered man must pay the penalty; if you rescue him, you will have to do it again" (Proverbs 19:19, NIV).

Let's be absolutely clear: this is a time of crisis in your life. Like the biblical patriarchs before you, you need to prepare for your journey and decide what you must bring and what you must leave behind. Many women who have been in your situation froze in their tracks as they contemplated what they might lose, the change in lifestyle they'd have to endure, the chaos to come, the uncertainty of when it would finally end. But you are running for your life. Remember Lot's wife. This is no time to look back.

While you can use *some* of the planning information above, you've got to keep it as simple as possible, as you're already aware of what actions would prompt suspicion and more abuse. Keep your planning notes at a friend's house. I would advise against looking through the household financial information if he is very controlling about it. *The most important thing you need is a safe place where you and your children can live.* Get a local yellow pages directory, and look under "Community Services." In that section you'll find listings for "abuse and family violence." You may also find local "safe house" shelters, information help lines, and other free services. If you can't do that, call the National Domestic Violence Hotline at 800-799-7233, toll free. This hotline or the other service agencies will help you form a plan to exit, a plan for your and your children's safety on a long-term basis. They have experience regarding the necessary evidence of abuse to collect, how and when to contact authorities for arrest or restraining orders, and more. Find a safe telephone and make the call. Or if your situation won't allow you to do the research, ask a friend to do it. Abuse never goes away on its own; it only escalates. No matter what your husband has told you, you are not to blame. And you are not alone. One in three American women has experienced domestic violence at the hands of her male partner. Three women in America die *every day* due to physical violence from their mates (see EndAbuse.org for more). Don't allow fear of more abuse to keep you from action. Your husband's strength is no match when you are following God's lead for your protection.

He will protect his godly ones, but the wicked shall be silenced in darkness.
No one shall succeed by strength alone. (1 Samuel 2:9)

In-House Separation

This arrangement works only when the husband is very motivated to repair his life and his marriage and the wife is somewhere between undecided and hopeful. In-house separation involves much less disruption to your daily life, but it is harder to maintain boundaries, since everything looks the same. It's of paramount importance to determine new rules for the house, the relationship, and your personal needs. Though the rules of in-house separation have been firmly set and agreed upon, there's no guarantee your husband will abide by them without a more drastic change: asking him to move out. But to give your in-house separation the best chance for success, you need to communicate and have agreement on:

- where each of you will sleep
- what household services will or will not be forthcoming
- physical boundaries for touch
- times to be together
- how/where you each spend your evenings
- what you expect of him and your goal for the separation

It's also fair to say that where there's anger or lack of motivation to change, the probability of a productive in-house separation is exceptionally low. The movie *The War of the Roses* is a good example of a poorly conceived in-house separation. If you haven't seen the movie in a while, you may want to watch it again and learn what not to do.

MY · STONE · WORK

Insight

As stated previously, feelings and circumstances change with time, but determine what choice you need to make for now, based on God's perspective and wise counsel rather than emotion. "Plans go wrong with too few counselors; many counselors bring success" (Proverbs 15:22).

- If your husband is safe to communicate with, tell him of any decision you've made to change direction.
- Turn your decision into a plan, using the suggestions above.
- Write down the terms on which you'll choose to stay, or if you're separating, write down the specific terms for reuniting, using the list of changes in the next section ("When to End Separation") as a template.
- If separation is your choice, determine a deadline for him to move out. One week is adequate for him to find at least a temporary situation. If you want him to leave immediately, agree to a time for him to come back to collect more of his belongings. If there is any concern for bad behavior on his part, have a male relative at the house when he comes. If he is unwilling to move out, make plans to leave, giving yourself a deadline as your goal. It becomes much more complicated if you have children and you are the one moving, but try to be out within a few weeks.
- Even if you feel at this time that you are certain you will choose divorce, it's often wise to separate for six months before taking legal action other than protecting financial assets. Follow the previously outlined details for planning a separation. Then wait, pray, and watch for what happens.

Action

Carry out your plan. Ask your walking companion to help you be accountable for acting on it and continue to prayerfully listen to God's voice in the matter. If you are considering a change in plans, ask yourself and your walking companion whether it's possible that fear is influencing you. Write down the things, good or bad, that are influencing your thinking.

When to End Separation

Visible, measurable changes need to occur before restoring the relationship. A women motivated to restore her marriage must not make a hasty reconciliation when she gets an apology or sees he's joined a men's group. It is absolutely critical for women to be patient and allow the separation to do its work. Use this checklist to ensure a reunion is not premature. The items in the left column are hopeful signs, but they can also be empty of sincerity. But coupled with the items in the right column, there is strong evidence of true change.

Positive Gestures That Don't Require Real Change	Consistent Behavior Indicative of Heart Change
☐ apologizes / asks for forgiveness	☐ stops blaming you for his behavior ☐ has humility of spirit, a contrite heart ☐ stops rationalizing his behavior ☐ shows true brokenness and repentance
☐ attends church regularly	☐ is applying teaching to his life
☐ joins men's support group	☐ does his homework ☐ is accountable to you and his group ☐ spends time in Bible study and prayer
☐ expresses a desire to be back together	☐ is patient; doesn't demand time line ☐ understands your need to feel safe ☐ is responsible for your financial needs
☐ insists he has changed	☐ is respectful of your feelings and needs ☐ is transparent about his schedule ☐ has worked on a budget plan with you ☐ old red flags aren't flying
☐ says he will do whatever it takes to get better	☐ you witness him going through the painful process of recovery ☐ is seeking God at every point of need ☐ is submitted to his pastor and men's group leaders ☐ pride, blame, and anger are diminished

Words and small gestures must be followed up with consistent action. How long is long enough to be certain? Have you done this dance before? Have you heard the same rhetoric? Did you end up in the same mess again? If you are tired of this dance, exercise patience until you see that your husband's changes are lasting.

Not So Fast!

What are some indicators that he is not interested in changing? Here are some common responses to separation from a husband who is not committed to changing himself or his relationship with you and the children:

- While you've been separated, it has become harder for him to stay in recovery.
- He calls separation "kicking him out."
- He's had "dates."
- His anger has not changed or has escalated.
- He's not concerned or responsible for your or your children's provision.
- He finds fault with and complains about his recovery group.
- He badgers you to set a date when he can come home.
- He uses gifts to manipulate a desired response from you.
- He demands forgiveness and trust.
- He only spends time with the children as a means to get an audience with you.
- He suggests divorce.

There are many other manipulating behaviors that indicate an unrepentant heart, but certainly if you're seeing any behavior that matches this list, be patient and let the separation do its work.

> O Lord, you will take naught but the truth. You have tried to get them to be honest,
> for you have punished them, but they won't change!… They refuse to turn from
> their sins. They are determined, with faces hard as rock, not to repent. (Jeremiah 5:3)

Attaining the Desired Outcome

As you spend many months separated, the primary focus—after getting peace back in your life—is gaining perspective. Is your husband truly a new person? Or is he still trying to manipulate his way through life? If you are watching and listening closely to him and those you have entrusted to support you through this process, you should begin to have clarity in time. You may ask, *If we are separated, how can I tell what is really going on?* You should have regularly scheduled meetings with your husband in a safe environment to discuss the family's current events, the children, and your individual states of mind and emotions.

When you believe you are witnessing "a new person" in front of you, get confirmation from others who are less invested in wanting a specific outcome. Seek the Holy Spirit, your walking companion, and other trusted friends, a pastor, or counselors to affirm your assessment. Remember, "in the multitude of counselors there is safety" (Proverbs 11:14, NKJV).

Often when we want something, we are reluctant to see that reality is not offering the thing we want. So we reject the reality and keep looking in the same place for different answers. Stay firmly planted in reality. Getting back together, yet finding yourself in the same old place, will be twice as painful. Sometimes setting a strong boundary, such as separation, will clarify a painful truth: that you were left a long time ago…in every way, perhaps, except physically. Acceptance of reality is the first step to healing your pain.

My Prayer for This Time of Separation

Lord, You know what my desire for this marriage is. I pray that the distance and time spent away from each other will be used to allow You full access to do a work in my husband's heart and mine. Give me strength to stay the course. Help me get through day by day in Your strength, not in my weakness. Show me how to make wise, loving, godly decisions. In Jesus's name, amen.

What's Really Possible

There's a good chance that at this point you're wondering, *What's reasonable for me to expect from this restoration project? Will I ever truly be whole again? Will he ever truly be whole again, or should I lower my expectations?*

Fred and Brenda, Clay and I, have walked, crawled, hiked, and run this obstacle course from total devastation to complete restoration. Not long ago we both crossed the landmark of our twenty-fifth anniversaries. Given the great challenges we have each persevered through, there is a richer essence to our celebrations. But the great news is that we are not just two "lucky" couples who got a golden ticket. The same result is available to all.

We have encountered thousands of couples who have done the same, healing their personal wounds, their marriages, and their children's trust in the exclusive union of marriage. Imagine Brenda and Fred's excitement as they recently watched their twenty-three-year-old son get married, having saved the first kiss for the altar.

I want to assure you that there is hope. Will your husband ever be truly victorious? If he's motivated, it can happen. Remember, God is in the restoration business, and He's relentless. If He can change our families' destinies, He can change yours as well.

It's certainly tough for men in our sensual society. Yet in spite of porn's pestilence, men can learn to defend themselves and develop a passion for purity. King David knew this hope, and he offers it to anyone trusting God and chasing hard after purity: "A thousand may fall at your side, ten thousand at your right hand, but it will not come near you" (Psalm 91:7, NIV).

Your husband can stand again. Your family can stand again. Part of it depends on how far you are willing to go with God to make that happen. What could happen in your heart and your home if you risked loving your husband as God does?

Women often say, "But after all this, I'm not even sure I know what normal looks like!" Brenda Stoeker paints this picture for us:

> I feel incredible security knowing that I'm married to a man who keeps his eyes to himself. Even after four babies and twenty-four years of aging together, I live unthreatened by any women around me. Fred loves me for me and is very satisfied with who I am and what I've become.
>
> When my husband prays, I'm confident that nothing is hindering his connection with God. If I knew of dark, hidden areas, I'd have no faith that his prayers would even rise to the ceiling, but I've seen how a pure man's prayer packs a spiritual punch.
>
> My confidence in Fred's spiritual protection is unbounded. I never wonder if there are open cracks in our spiritual defenses where the Enemy can slip into our lives. Christianity is not a game to Fred, and image means nothing. He'd rather *be* a Christian than seem like one....
>
> He's proven in battle that his commitment to the Lord and his love for his family are the highest priorities in his life....
>
> This normal, godly pattern leaves everyone flourishing, and this wouldn't be possible if blatant sin were clogging things up. I know who Fred is, and in the secret places of life, I know where he will not go. (*Every Heart Restored*, 189)

So go back to the original question. What is really possible to achieve during a restoration project like this? Every good thing we need.

Though none of us have guarantees about our circumstances in this life, we can choose to hold on to God's hope-filled promise for the days ahead: " 'For I know the plans I have for you,' declares the LORD, 'plans to prosper you and not to harm you, plans to give you hope and a future' " (Jeremiah 29:11, NIV).

Even if your husband doesn't change, you can. Though I trust Clay, my security isn't based on him. The biggest work God did in me was teaching me to rest in the knowledge that I can trust in His infallibility, that He will take care of me no matter what path Clay takes.

But again, there are no guarantees. My trust in God's goodness will strengthen me even if Clay precedes me in death. The strength God gave me to be fearless about the future was separate from the restoration of our marriage. This same trust also allows me to love Clay for the man he is now, without holding back for fear that I could be hurt again.

Ultimately, one question remains: will you choose to trust and follow God's good plans to rebuild your life despite what your husband may choose?

The Journey Continues

This twelve-week guidebook is not the end of the journey. As you may realize, there's more vital work still to do. I don't want you to miss out on the next essential parts of your journey, so I hope you'll obtain volume 2 of *The Healing Choice Guidebook* and continue your healing.

For without a doubt, the most important thing to hold on to throughout this process is hope. That God-woven rope is braided from the many things you've released to Him up to this point. As you continue on, remember to cling not to your old life or the things you've lost and can't control but simply to that life-giving rope. Hope is the answer for getting through the next hour, or the next year, regardless of the circumstances. I want to encourage you that healing of a marriage is truly possible with two who are willing to surrender. But there's also surpassing hope for you if your husband is unwilling. I have witnessed the rebirth of women's lives, full of joy and contentment, though the husbands were no longer in the picture. All women can be healed and restored to joy, despite their husband's behaviors, by the One True Source. Keys to finding that joy, hope, healing, and richness of life are contained in the next volume.

In that guidebook, we will pick up the topic of how to pray powerfully and strategically for your marriage, how to fully release the outcome of your situation, and how submission can work when your marriage isn't working. We'll take an in-depth look at how a man changes and what exactly that looks like, discuss how to explain things to your children, and tell you how to do all you can to prevent sexual dysfunction from being passed on. We'll also look at the specific ways you can get your unique unmet needs and desires answered when your husband isn't available. There is much more to learn and process on this journey, including the secret to recapturing joy in your life and pinpointing your next steps from there.

For now, I hope you'll continue the journey, making healing choices, accompanied by your walking companions and your heavenly Father. May you always reach for the God of hope as your lifeline on this journey. I look forward to sharing the rest of the journey with you.

Help Pave the Way for Others

From the abundance of your heart, your Avenue group thrives. Avenue group participants continue to be the primary source of financial support for starting new groups. We continually strive to bring you the highest quality program available. Your contributions fund ongoing training and encouragement for your facilitators. Donations make more groups possible, so we hope that as you are blessed by this resource, you will consider participating in giving back as a valued member. Some groups facilitate the collection of your weekly contribution; some don't. If you have found this study helpful, please consider making your contribution through AvenueResource.com.

Acknowledgments

To my good friends and pastors, Ron and Susan Pinkston of East Bay Fellowship, Danville, California, thank you for your prayers, love, wisdom, and encouragement. I greatly admire you for so bravely going where many pastors won't tread. Without you, this ministry would not exist.

To Kris Phillips, my deepest gratitude for your investment in my life as a friend and unknowingly as a mentor. I've learned how a real friend behaves. You saw me through some very dark days and remain one of my richest earthly treasures.

To my many friends whom God placed in my life when I finally surrendered to His wooing, You shared of your own pain and failures when I was in the depths of mine. Knowing that I was among people who were willing to risk being real helped me to take off my veil of secrecy. It was with you that I learned to live an authentic life. For that I am continually thankful.

To the many women I've had the privilege of getting to know, and being known by, as I facilitated those first groups. I've learned so much from you, which added depth and dimension to this guidebook. There is such a bond of sisterhood among us. Though our paths cross only intermittently, it's always like seeing an old friend who knows all about you and loves you anyway.

To Sandy Fraser and Gail Wood, who took my "baby" in their arms and continued to nurture the first Avenue women's chapter when I moved into the "author" phase of my life.

To my mother, Frances Kelley, and my mother-in-law, Joan Allen, for your continual love and prayers.